# CONFESSIONS OF A TRADESMAN

## WORKS BY THE SAME AUTHOR

WITH CHRIST AT SEA.   Crown 8vo, Cloth, 6s.

A WHALEMAN'S WIFE.   Crown 8vo, Cloth, 6s.

THE APOSTLES OF THE SOUTH-EAST.   Crown 8vo, Cloth, 6s.

SEA SPRAY.   Crown 8vo, Cloth, 6s.

ADVANCE AUSTRALASIA.   Crown 8vo, Cloth, 6s.

LONDON: HODDER & STOUGHTON

# CONFESSIONS OF
# A TRADESMAN

BY

## FRANK T. BULLEN

AUTHOR OF
"WITH CHRIST AT SEA," "THE CRUISE OF THE CACHALOT"
ETC.

HODDER AND STOUGHTON
LONDON MCMVIII

*Printed in* 1908

To

THE SMALL TRADESMEN

OF LONDON

# PREFACE

IT is a particular, and not altogether pleasant, feature of literary work in Britain that should an author make a certain amount of success with a book on one particular topic, it is thenceforward tacitly assumed that he must stick to that topic, assaying no other on pain of being mercilessly taken to task by the critics. Or what is worse, damned with faint praise. With this knowledge very vividly impressed upon me, I have hitherto refrained from writing upon a subject with which I have most intimate and painful acquaintance, and one that should appeal to a far wider circle of readers than any of my previous books have done. It is the subject of the small, struggling tradesman or shop-keeper.

I may, I trust, be permitted to remind my good friends, the public, to whom I owe so great a debt, that prior to going to sea I was, as some writers love to say, not entirely unconnected with trade, having for two or three years been employed with varying degrees of unsuccess by small tradesmen as an errand boy, etc. In this wise (although I feel sure that none of my employers would have suspected me of it), I absorbed some germs of a commercial spirit, did at any rate acquire the rudiments of trade, although in most irregular and entirely erratic ways.

During my sea-career, these germs lay entirely dormant, unfruitful; but they were undoubtedly tenacious of life, as we learn that disease germs always are; and so, when I forsook the sea upon an offer of a job ashore, a fitting environment aroused them, and they sprang into active life. Not of course immediately, a period of incubation was needed. It was readily forthcoming. At the age of twenty-five, I deliberately turned my back upon a profession that then offered me nothing better than mate of a tramp at £6 per month, and accepted a berth in a public office ashore at £2 per week, having a wife and one child, and no stick of furniture for a home.

Is it necessary to say that never having known any training in thrift, having indeed belonged to the least provident of all our notably improvident workers, I soon found the shoe pinching, soon discovered that forty shillings a week was devoid of elasticity, especially when curbed by payments to be made for furniture purchased on the very unsatisfactory " hire system "? Perhaps not, but in any case it was this,

coupled with the knowledge that all my fellow clerks
were driven by the necessities of their miserable pay
into bye-ways of supplementing their income, that
lured me back to trade again. Here let me digress
for a purpose. Many and grave scandals have been
unearthed in the Civil Service, note well, in the higher
branches even, but none I think greater than those
where poorly paid clerks toiled to do the work for
which their seniors were paid ; said seniors being
meanwhile engaged in amassing fortunes as eminent
authorities upon art, the drama, or sport. But in the
office where I was employed no such scandals were
possible, seeing that the pay of the most powerful
clerk therein was less than the annual tailor's bill
of some of the superior Civil Service clerks. And
whatever might be the value put upon our labours
by those without, it is at least incontrovertible that
we worked hard, so hard indeed that our superimposed
labours after hours in order to keep the domestic pot
boiling were cruel.

Of the manner of my escape from that Stygian lake
with all its monotony and despair of outlook, I have
perhaps said more than enough in print already,
and in any case it would here be quite out of place.
But of the time during which I in common with many
thousands of my fellows in London endeavoured to

live respectably, and rear a family by honest toil, I feel free to speak, and if incidentally I can throw a few side-lights, humorous or pathetic, as the case may be, upon the strenuous lives led by small London tradesmen, I shall be proportionately glad.

It only remains that while in the following pages fiction finds no place, no real names are given for the most obvious reasons.

FRANK T. BULLEN.

MILLFIELD,
  MELBOURN.

# CONTENTS

# CHAPTER I

## ENTERING BUSINESS

WITH the causes of my first plunge into the troubled waters of trade at the early age of nine I have here nothing to do. It must suffice to say that one spring morning, over forty years ago, I entered the emporium of an oil, colour, and Italian warehouseman (to quote from his fascia), in what was then known as Kensal New Town, a neighbourhood that had long been of unsavoury reputation, but was emerging into something like respectability by the aid of sundry long rows of jerry-built, stucco-ornamented houses, the inhabitants of which tried hard to forget the former appellation of their chosen abiding-place, and dated their letters, when they wrote any, from Upper Westbourne Park.

Mingled with the rows of mean streets of private dwellings were a few scattered shops tenanted by brave and daring folk who lived principally upon hope and a little capital. One of these had established himself between a butcher and a baker, and having laid in a stock of the amazingly miscellaneous description which characterises what we in London call

A

*tout court*, an " oil shop," awaited local custom. But having no children to assist him, and his wife being fully occupied with household duties, he sought additional help, and I obtained the situation. How vivid and fresh is the recollection of my opening morn ! With what awe did I gaze upon the closely packed shop, wondering however mortal mind could tell where everything was stowed; how curiously did I sniff the mingled odours of paint, soap, paraffin, glue, dog-biscuit, size, etc., all combined by the piney scent of the newly chopped wood which was stacked in halfpenny bundles up against the counter.

My employer was a stout, stern, dark man, who appeared to me like the dread arbiter of my fate, and his deep voice sent a thrill of apprehension through me as he gave me my first order, which was to carry home some wood, seven bundles for threepence, to one of the aristocracy of the vicinity. It was a heavy load for my thin arms, but had I been unable to lift it I should have strained myself to injury point in the endeavour to do so, such was my pride in my first commission. I wasted no time on the way, and ran back with the cash, triumphant, panting with exertion, pride, and the consciousness of ability.

Thenceforward I knew no idle moments, for my master was an expert in keeping me at it; he was never at a loss for a job for me, nor, to do him justice, did I ever see him idle himself. In fact, my only respite during the long day, from 7 A.M. till 10 P.M., was when, munching my crusts of bread and dripping, I minded the shop during his meal times, my mouth watering at the savoury smells which assailed my nostrils through all the reek of the shop, from his little parlour.

I have now a curious notion that I was too willing, because I know that I must have made him forget how puny an urchin I was, or he would never have sent me on the errands he did. One of these in the early days of my service with him stands out, salient, against the background of memory. It was in the early days of the Metropolitan Railway, which then ran only from Shepherd's Bush to Moorgate Street. There was a funny little primitive station at Westbourne Park, which was but a mile from our shop, and one day, giving me a few pence for my half-fare, he despatched me to Shoreditch to fetch something, I knew not what, for which he had given me an order in a sealed envelope. Proud as possible, I dashed off, took my ticket at Westbourne Park for the City, and arriving at Moorgate Street, inquired my way to Shoreditch, which I reached without any difficulty. A salesman took my order, looked at me, and said loftily, " Ow yer goin' ter take it ? " In reply I only stared dumbly, because I had no idea what " it " was. He shrugged his shoulders and retired, presently bringing forward an iron drum full of treacle, which he plumped before me, saying, " There y' are." I looked at it helplessly for a moment, and then looked at him ; but seeing no encouragement in his eye, essayed to lift it, and found that I could just manage to raise it an inch or two from the floor.

" Can't carry it," I said.

" Nothin' to do wi' me," he replied, taking it up—oh, so easily, I thought—and putting it outside on the pavement. I did not need telling what that meant, and so calling my wits to work, I did the best I knew, that is, I turned it over on its side and rolled it ! Yes, I rolled it along Shoreditch, up Worship Street, and along Finsbury Pavement, until I came opposite Moorgate Street Station, where I halted, baffled by the width of that great highway. But a kindly costermonger came to my aid, and, finding what the trouble was, uttered many strange words about the behaviour of whoever had sent such a kid on an errand of this kind ; then, hoisting the drum on his barrow, he wheeled it across the road and deposited it within the station. Thence I rolled it to the steps and managed to work it down them on to the plat-form (I am afraid I quite forgot to thank my kind helper), where it was lifted into the van by a sym-pathetic guard, and we rattled off to Westbourne Park. Arriving there, and being helped again by the tender-hearted guard aforesaid, I rolled my incubus into a dark corner, and fled shopwards, pantingly explaining on arrival that I wanted the " truck." Granted, with gloomy brows, by the boss.

Now this truck, of which more anon, was one of

those curiously shaped ones used exclusively by wine merchants at that time. It was curved and hollow, in order to take one barrel. It had a very long push handle, and no bottom. So you can imagine how difficult was my journey with that drum upon it, a veritable pilgrimage of pain. Let me pause awhile to solemnly curse that truck, and the evil chance that harnessed me to its awkwardness. Nevertheless upon this occasion I did reach my journey's end in safety, with the drum and its contents intact, only to be grumbled at because I had been so long!

But before I quit the subject of that truck, I must tell of my great exploit in connection with it. It was so entirely unhandy and unsuitable for general purposes, besides being so infernally heavy to push or pull that it was as much as I could do to handle it when empty. Yet I was so willing and eager that my employer forgot my pigmy size and put me to tasks absurdly beyond my strength, simply because he didn't think. I don't for a moment believe he was deliberately cruel or callous, and I know that although entirely free to do so, and often sorely aggravated, he never struck me, nor ever abused me. One day, however, he sent me on an errand to the older part of Kensal New Town with a hundredweight of bar soap in a box balanced on that truck. For some reason, which I forget, but probably hurry, he omitted to lash the box—it would have been a difficult operation in any case; and so I started off, trying to push the truck with one hand and hold the box on with the other, as the truck jolted over the stones—and succeeded fairly well too, until I came to a quagmire of a road where building was going on. Still I strove, the truck bumping horribly over the boulders hidden beneath the mud, until, when abreast of a church, which was just abuilding, the calamity which had been looming ever since I left the shop occurred—the box slid off the truck and capsized in the mud. The bars of soap flew in all directions, disposing themselves picturesquely as if planted in the slush, and I surveyed the awful scene in a sort of philosophic calm, feeling indeed that *kismet* had conquered me, and not carelessness or inefficiency. It never occurred to me to blame my employer.

From that stupor or reverie I was aroused by the loud laughter of the bricklayers on the scaffolding near at hand, and I sprang with desperate energy to the task of righting the wrong. First, I replaced the box, then, stripping off my little jacket, I disinterred bar after bar of the soap. I scraped the thick of the mud off on the side of the barrow, and then wiping the bars as clean as I could on my jacket, I replaced them one by one in the box, nor did I lose any. By the time I had finished, and I had no help, a circumstance which even now I wonder at—it would have been hard to tell which was muddiest, the truck, the box, the soap, or myself. But my only object being to get that box home, I took no heed of such an extrinsic matter as mud; and when, at last, I pushed off again with my cargo, I felt quite a glow of legitimate pride, for that I had retrieved my disaster.

How I escaped another before emerging from that bad road I do not know; but I did, and presently arrived at my destination, overheated, unrecognisable for mud, but triumphant. I knocked at the door, and the laundress appeared, a comely figure in spotless print. She gave a little start back when she saw me, as if she feared I would soil her eyesight, but I said quickly—

" Please, 'm, I've brought the soap."

She, incredulously, " Oh, 'ave yer! Well, it's abaht time. Bring it in."

I hastened to the barrow, loaded myself with an armful of bars, and hastened back. But she met me at the door, and glancing at my burden, put up her hand in protest, crying—

" What the devil d'ye call *that*."

" It's the soap, m'am," replied I meekly.

" Don't you dare bring none o' that muck in 'ere, young man," said she grimly.

Then I pleaded that a little scraping would make it all right, and used other feeble arguments, to all of which she presented a stony front, when suddenly our conference was interrupted by the appearance of my employer, who, with profuse apologies, wheeled away the soap, leaving me to follow, but apparently caring not whether I did. I felt terribly guilty as I followed him back, and never dreamed of blaming him for the catastrophe. I have often wondered since whether he blamed himself.

Be that as it may, I remember he said no word as we twain unloaded the sombre cargo and scraped each bar with utter care, making the scrapings into a ball. It was a long job, for customers kept coming in for pennyworths of soap, and halfpenny bundles of wood, and farthingsworths of blacking, at which trivial interruptions he still evinced no irritability, but when at last all was finished he weighed the ball of scrapings and found it equivalent to three bars and a half of soap. These he added to the pile of cleansed bars, repacked them, and started me off again, warning me, however, to go a long way round in order to avoid the road where I had come to grief; and on Saturday night he stopped the value of that soap out of my week's wages, which left me 2s., for I was then receiving 4s. per week.

As I lived with a laundress, I was able to make a bargain for the ball of soap-scrapings, so managed to scrape through, though not without difficulty and many cursory remarks upon my behaviour. Now, as if my troubles were not sufficient, the baker's and butcher's boys on either side conceived a dislike to me, and lost no opportunity of making my life a burden, especially when, during spells of leisure in the evenings, I watched the store of pails, crockery, etc., arranged outside the shop. Many and harsh were the tricks they played on me, until I discovered that they both smoked, and thenceforward I purchased immunity from persecution with handfuls of shag tobacco, purloined from the back of the counter while the boss was inside at his meals, not recking of the risk I ran, in view of present ease.

My experiences altogether were of an exceedingly varied character in this business, and I must often have made my employer feel that life was hardly worth living when my blunders were frequent and painful; yet, on the whole, I feel that he had his full money's worth out of me—especially on Saturday nights, when the shop would be full, mostly of urchins carrying all sorts of utensils and yelling " pint er penny oy-el," in twenty different keys all at once, while almost everybody watched an opportunity to steal a bundle of wood or some other trifling article. Once, indeed, a purblind old woman put a bundle of wood in her basket abstractedly, not noticing that it had a piece of thin string fast to it, and methinks I can now see her amazed face as on nearing the door the string grew tight and jerked her plunder out of the basket along with some other small parcels. But my governor was equal to the occasion. He said calmly—

" I don't think I took for that bundle, m'am, and you somehow got hold of the wrong one," quietly putting it back and handing her another, which she took, and forked out the halfpenny.

But after about four months matters reached a climax. I was sent hurriedly to Paddington one night for a box of tallow candles of about ten pounds' weight, with urgent orders to hurry, as the stock was out. I did hurry. On the way back, running down Brindley street with the box on my head, I stumbled, and the box flew off into the road with a crash. It did not break, so I snatched it up and ran off again. Arriving at the shop all breathless, I found three customers waiting to be served with candles. The boss seized the box, burst it open, and, lo! there was not a whole candle within! He glared at me, but refrained from expressing any opinion. Apologising to his customers, he dismissed them candleless. Then turning to me, he said, with an effort, " You'll go on Saturday. And take those candles for your week's wages. I've had enough of *you*." And probably he had.

Incidentally, I may mention that the laundress with whom I lived, and for whom I worked when out of a job, resented intensely my bringing home those candles in lieu of four shillings, and I suffered many things until the last of those mutilated lumps of tallow and cotton had been disposed of.

I spent about a month of misery working in the laundry at night, and by day looking for a job, until I obtained a situation at a boot-shop in Archer Street, Notting Hill, as errand-boy, my wages being 3s. 6d. per week and my tea. Here my opportunities for blundering were fewer, the business being so much more simple. My duties were to run errands, dust the shop, and keep the floor clean. I was really much better off than before, though the hours were very long, till ten every night but Saturday, and then till midnight; for my work was not heavy, and the good meal I got every evening was a great help. But I confess sadly that, all my earnings going for my lodgings, I devised a dishonest plan for getting a little pocket-money. When taking home the repairs, I would add threepence or sixpence to the price, and when my scheme panned out all right, as it often did, I pocketed the difference. But of course I was soon discovered, and literally kicked out by my irate employer, who stigmatised me as a young thief, and spoke of prison and the policeman, whom I dreaded far more.

I pass over the weary time of waiting for another job, when indeed I worked far harder than while in a place, and come to my next billet, which was at a trunk-maker's in the Edgware Road. Whether my employer was the owner of the business or not I never knew, but, as I remember him, he was more like a soulless automaton than a man. He employed no one but me in the huge shop, and only one man in the workshop below, who was principally at work making, that is covering, ladies' dress-baskets. Every morning at eight, after hoisting the revolving shutters with a winch handle, I toiled, with occasional assistance from the governor, in building up a huge pile of trunks, bags, boxes, etc., outside the shop, a pile which was made more imposing by a great, black, box-like thing, about ten feet long by three feet square, which he used to help me lug in and out.

He lived in a little den in one corner of the shop, and made his meals of tea (which he made over the gas-flame by which he wrote) and bread and butter, which I fetched for him, a twopenny coburg, and two ounces of fourteenpenny Dorset at a time. Never once did he speak a kind or considerate word to me, or even offer me a crust of his bread—no, he used to save and soak them and eat them himself; at which I wondered and grumbled secretly, for I felt that he could well afford to leave me a few scraps, as I was always hungry. But 'twas not i' the bond.

I had very little to do here in the way of errand-running, but I had no idle moments, and when not occupied in the almost interminable job of dusting the stock and cleaning out the shop, I could always find work below, making paste and lining the cheap boxes we made for servants. And here I was quite happy, for the journeyman was a genial soul and beguiled the time with jokes and snatches of song, often too giving me a portion of his frugal dinner or a halfpenny, which I promptly invested in " broken stale " at the baker's hard by, where I purchased the governor's coburgs.

But it was a dull, hard, monotonous life, and only for the fact that I occasionally got hold of a copy of the

" Boys of England," " The Young Briton," or the "Sons
of Britannia," among the waste-paper we used for
linings, and lost myself in the realms of romance with
" Caradoc the Briton," " Alone in the Pirate's Lair,"
or the " Young Centurion," there would have been
hardly a gleam of sunshine in my young life. Those
blessed stories supplied the place of pleasant companions and of kind words, and were in a great
measure educational—at any rate, they were all the
schooling in one sense that I had.

I had been at this slow business several months,
when one day my employer, without thinking, I am
sure, of what he was doing, sent me to Hoxton to
fetch a full-sized leather portmanteau from one of the
small workers who make such things at home. Of
course he gave me no money for travelling, my time
at four shillings a week was not valuable, and off I set.
Arriving at my journey's end, and stating my errand,
the man handed the article to me, that is he put it
outside his door, and left me to deal with it as best I
could. Now, it was so large that I could almost have
got into it, and it was correspondingly heavy. But
I was six miles from home, and had to do something ;
so, as I could not lift it, I started to drag it along the
pavement through a light, drizzling rain. Coming to
an oil-shop, I went in and begged a yard of clothes-
line, which I rove through the handle, and, incredible
as it may appear, I actually *towed* that portmanteau
home. I was nearly four hours doing that six miles,

and reached the shop late in the evening, dead beat, but triumphant.

It was a short-lived triumph, though, for that spruce portmanteau looked as if it had been subjected to years of the hardest wear, and was besides almost covered with mud. My employer gave one glance at it, uttered a sort of whoop, and sat down trembling. I stood facing him, wondering what would happen. Suddenly he rose and uttered his nightly formula, " Close the establishment."

As soon as that heavy task was done, he placed two shillings in my hand (it was Wednesday night), and said, " If ever you come near this shop again, and I catch you, I'll break every bone in your skin." I said, " Good night, sir," and fled, pleased to think I had escaped so easily. And thus abruptly ended my acquaintance with the trunk-maker's art. Hitherto, it must be confessed, I had made no great hit at commerce, not even having been able to obtain a character. But I suppose I was an unconscious opportunist, for I wasted little energy in vain regrets, but cast about for a new opening after each phase of experience.

# CHAPTER II

## CONTINUED TROUBLE

BY some strange freak of good fortune to which I was totally unaccustomed, the very next day after my summary dismissal from the trunk-maker's, I got a job in a big dairy company's business. I have forgotten exactly how it happened, but I think that one of my street chums told me he had seen the notice in the shop window, and hurrying off at once, I secured the situation. At first blush I was almost overwhelmed with the magnitude of my good fortune. For my wages were to be six shillings per week, and a pint of milk twice a day, which to me was wealth indeed, and I began to have visions of getting a little pocket-money out of my earnings, and perhaps even, blissful thought, a new suit of clothes, a possession that I had never yet enjoyed.

My delight was somewhat tempered by the fact that my hours of business were to be from 4.30 A.M. to 9 P.M., on Sunday and week-day alike, in summer ; and from 5.30 A.M. to 9 P.M. in winter. But of course that was merely a detail. As I had to begin at so unholy an hour in the morning, of course it was unthinkable that I could get any food in the house, and so my landlady made arrangements, in consideration of receiving the whole of my earnings *and* the milk, to subsidise a local coffee-stall keeper to the extent of one cup of coffee and one slice of cake, price together one penny, every morning. This I bolted at the street corner, often scalding my mouth, for I need hardly say that the margin of time was never very great. And if a boy arrived late, well, there was an end, for his van had gone without him, since it might not linger, obstructing the others.

After swallowing my coffee, I fled as fast as my legs would carry me towards my place of business (sounds important, doesn't it ?), which, when I reached it, was a roaring vortex of noise. For the railway vans had just arrived from Paddington Station, and the huge churns of milk were being shifted with much clangour and shouting from the street to the cellar of the shop, where their contents were being distributed into the polished churns which went into the distributing vans. Every man and boy was hard at work, the majority fitting out their respective vans with cans, kettles, etc. ; and in half an hour from beginning this work, every van (there were sixteen of them) with its driver and its attendant boy, a crate full of empty cans, and two brimming churns of milk, had rattled off towards the district, often three or four miles away, which was allotted to it.

In summer this eager rush and excitement was rather

pleasant, and more in the nature of a huge frolic than otherwise; but in winter, on bitter, bleak, snowy, or wet mornings, it was undoubtedly terribly hard upon such children as I, poorly clad and insufficiently fed, as most of us were. There were two of us in my van besides the driver, it being a *heavy* district, and there was consequently considerable rivalry between my fellow-worker and myself, which kept both of us from lagging. Our boss was a gruff, unsociable sort of fellow, but he must have had a soft spot in his heart somewhere, for he invariably pulled up at the first coffee stall (it was set against a dead wall, nearly opposite the entrance to Kensington Palace Gardens, I remember), and treated each of us to a pennyworth of coffee and cake; and this kindness he repeated when we had finished our round, if the weather was cold.

Upon arriving at the commencement of our district we at once flew into violent activity, distributing the milk in cans down the areas and at the doors; but at seven we began to serve at the doors, the servants being about, and many a chunk of cake and mug of hot coffee fell to my lot from kind-hearted kitchen-maids. So, taking it all round, it was not entirely unpleasant if very exhausting. But one thing I have never been able to understand, the wonderful memory we developed. We carried no books, and yet when we returned to the shop at about eight, each of us went before the cashier and repeated, without an

B

effort apparently, as he read out the numbers of the houses, the quantity of milk we had served them with. I do not remember learning this, and indeed it seemed to come naturally to all of us. And when it is remembered that out of 150 gallons of milk we were only allowed one quart for margin, it can easily be understood that we must have been pretty correct.

We had an hour allowed for breakfast, and then the boys had to return and wash and polish the big cans or kettles, as we called them, a task which took us till the afternoon, when we sallied forth again in all the glory of white smocks, shining cans, and trim equipages. This was the pleasant time, for there were nice little snacks obtainable at kitchen doors, and many an opportunity of making a dishonest halfpenny by selling milk to strangers, which deficiency in our pails we made up by giving short measure to regular and large customers, but never, as far as I know, by calling in the aid of the pump. At night when we returned, and the men took their vans off to the stables, the boys washed up the hundreds of small cans under the acute supervision of an old foreman. All the cans were washed and rinsed, were stacked with open lids ready for the morning, and at about 9.30 we were released.

I do not know how long this strenuous employment claimed me, but I know that I was one day discharged suddenly without explanation. The only reason I can assign is that some of my petty pilferings of milk had been discovered, and the only excuse I can give is that of all my earnings I never had a halfpenny to call my own—it all went for my keep.

Why or how I went to my next place I shall never know. It is to me and always has been a profound mystery. It was at a "lath-render's," a place where laths were made by hand from curved fillets of Russian pine, with a groove down the centre as if showing whence the pith had been removed, that had often aroused my wonder as to their use. I was to receive, as far as I remember, small wages, and certainly no food, but I was to learn the business! But my only occupation while I was there was to tie up chips for sale and keep the fire going in the stove, although I watched the men splitting the long laths from the billets with a sort of hatchet with keenest interest. Ah, yes, I used to saw the billets into lengths, I remember, but not to any extent. I was too small for such strenuous labour.

Well, my whole course there is misty in retrospect, but deeply flavoured with the pleasant scent of the pine wood, except the manner of my leaving, which was sudden, dramatic, and mysterious. I have said that my principal occupation was the tying up of chips. There were naturally a great many of these, and they were made into bundles by the aid of a rude machine, and sold, largely to laundresses, who used to send for them as being more economical than the bundle-wood at the oil-shops. Now what perverse demon tempted me I know not, but one day I thought it would be a desirable thing to conceal in the heart of each bundle a lump of clinker from the stove ! No possible benefit could accrue to me from doing this, and had my reasoning powers been in working order, I must have known that detection and subsequent disaster must inevitably be swift.

But I did not think, and I did include clinkers in my bundles, with the result that one day a horde of infuriated washerwomen, mostly of Irish extraction, descended upon the shop armed with clinkers, with which, after briefest prologue, they pelted my unfortunate and totally innocent employer. He, poor man, could do nothing but close the establishment under this rapid fire of missiles; and then, thinking quickly, turned upon me and flung me out, not, I rejoice to say, as a sacrifice to the mob, but by a rear door, whence I escaped along the canal side. Explanation of my conduct I have none, and there I must leave the matter. It may have been the budding of incipient genius, but in the mellow light of retrospect I confess that it appears very like the act of a lunatic of which I had been guilty.

Again, I was free and still characterless. This time I suffered, as no doubt I deserved, hunger, thirst, and pain before I again entered employment, but when I did get a berth it promised fairer than any of my previous ones. Just how I fell in with this astounding piece of luck, I have forgotten, but what is indelibly impressed upon my memory is the fact that in my new situation I received board and clothing and two shillings a week—quite sufficient to pay for my poor little bed in a room which I shared with a cobbler, who used it for a workshop, toiling far into the night after I had gone to sleep; but while I was awake, entertaining me vastly with scraps of quaint philosophy. No wonder I was what they used to call an old-fashioned kid! But bless that dear old cobbler's heart. He was gentle, kind, and wise, except in one direction, but even in his cups I never remember hearing him say ought that a little child might not listen to, or ask and obtain the meaning of unsullied. He was very fond of me, and I of him. I daresay we meant a great deal to each other, meeting as we did in that little eddy out of the great rapids of life, and without visible effort supplying each other's needs. I well remember meeting him one day—it must have been when I was looking for a job—surrounded by a little mob of children " avin a gime wiv im " in the vernacular. Taking me gently by the arm he said, with a grand wave of his free hand, " Now here is an example for you, ill-mannered brats that you are, that can only shout ' 'Ullo, Trotty.' I know I trot, I know I am old, but you are ill-bred to remind me of it, and as for this dear child ! " And much to my horror and entire discomfiture, he lifted me up and kissed me.

I did not get over that, or escape the consequences of his ill-timed affection for a long time, I promise you.

But I am forgetting Mr Green, my employer. He kept an establishment in Westbourne Grove for the manufacture and sale of paper patterns of fashionable dresses. In those far-off days I think he must have been a pioneer in this business, and I know he used to visit Paris periodically, in order to obtain the latest modes; and returning with them, his wife and her assistants reduplicated them in coloured paper, which elaborate models were exhibited in a grand show-room and sold. My business was to wear a fine suit of clothes with many silvered buttons, and lie hidden in the hall to conduct clients upstairs to the show-rooms, which was on the first floor over a shop. Another and more important part of my duties was to carry parcels to clients' houses, at which times I wore a shiny top-hat bedecked with silver braid. Indeed, so fine was I that my old companions of the street forbore to guy me, but paid me undisguised tribute of admiration for my splendour.

At such times as I was not employed in public work as aforesaid, I assisted the housemaid in her domestic duties, and was indeed a boy of all work. But taking it all round, I had a good place, and but for the one defect of never having any money of my own, I might have remained there until I began to grow a beard. But I could not resist the temptation of pilfering, because I had never anything of my own, and so in spite of my comfort and ease I forfeited this good place, and was suddenly kicked out. I had not yet, it will be seen, discovered for myself that honesty was the best policy, and I was certainly not one of those wonderful children of whom we read in prize-books that they would starve rather than steal. I stole whenever I saw a favourable opportunity, and when found out and made to suffer therefor, only blamed my own stupidity in not taking more elaborate precautions.

My next employment was at a chemist's, and my never ending wonder is, that I am alive to tell of my experiences there. For it was a large business, and they employed a light porter, a big boy of about eighteen, to do the work I was too weak for; and this fellow led me on to sample portions of the stock, which exercise on several occasions nearly proved fatal to me. But my direst experience was not due to him at all. I was sent one day with a basket containing six syphons of soda to a client's house in Inverness Place, and at the corner of Inverness Terrace, where it joins the Place, I, resting, saw a fellow errand-boy approaching. After salutations, he suddenly caught sight of my burden as I sat upon the handle of the basket, and immediately asked me why I did not have a drink, and give him some. I, who knew nothing of syphons and their peculiarities, scoffed at the idea. But he very seriously gave me to understand that soda water was a kind of sublimated lemonade, and that it was most easy to get out of these patent bottles, which indeed were made for the purpose.

I needed little persuasion to try the experiment, and so in a minute or two behold me kneeling on the pavement, while that fiend, taking out one of the syphons, inserted the spout in my mouth, and telling me to draw hard, pulled the trigger ! Merciful powers, shall I, can I, ever forget the agony of that moment ! I felt the impact of that surcharged stream against my diaphragm, and simultaneously a regurgitating flood seemed to be beating against my skull, while a double stream poured down my nostrils. He, the miscreant, yelling with delight, dropped the syphon on the pavement and fled, leaving me three parts dead, with a charge against me of something like five shillings and sixpence for a broken syphon. Fun to him doubtless, but to me ! ! !

I must pass rapidly over several other adventures at that fatal shop, such as my putting a handful of soft soap in my mouth in mistake for honey, and exuding soapsuds from every pore for hours as it seemed, eating greedily of ipecacuanha lozenges and worm tablets, both given me by the light porter, with equally disastrous results, until one fateful Saturday night came with the remark from the manager as he handed me my four shillings and sixpence, that I was too volatile for his business, and that as he did not want a post-mortem on the premises, I had better not trouble to return on Monday morning. Which valediction I received as quite in keeping with the recognised scheme of things as far as I was concerned.

But I could not help feeling that a crisis in my affairs had arrived, and I dared not return to my lodging with the now too familiar remark, " I've got the sack," so forgathering with another boy, similarly situated, I cut loose from such conventionalities as I had hitherto preserved; and after a riotous expenditure of sixpence in fried fish and chips and gingerbeer, we climbed the railings of Kensington Gardens, and creeping like Indians through the gloom, ensconced ourselves within the shrubbery by the Serpentine under a heap of plant matting, and slept soundly till morning.

That was the beginning of an Arab life in the great city, which, I suppose, must have had a certain charm for me, in that it was made up almost entirely of exciting episodes, tempered by the two salient factors of cold and hunger. I can never remember being warm and well fed together for more than an hour or two at a time, and those occasions were so rare as to mark their occurrence indelibly as periods to be reckoned from. I had no prevision, no ambition except to get a good feed and a warm place to sleep, no anxiety save to avoid the policeman, for the School Board Official was not yet in existence, nor as far as I was aware, any other person whose business it was to look after waifs and strays such as I was.

Now, curiously enough, one fact stands out in great prominence for which I cannot account at all. It will have been noticed that I had, to put it mildly, no excessive scruples as to taking what did not belong to me, if I thought I needed it ; but one thing I would not, could not, did not do, was beg. In the whole of that adventurous time of which I am writing, and afterwards when I was stranded in strange places between voyages in the early days, although I often suffered most acute pangs of hunger, I never once asked alms. And that, I think, will be found quite characteristic of the London street boy. It is a curious, and, I think, not unsatisfactory feature in his make-up. But there is no denying that we were all predatory in the highest degree. And this habit grew upon us, well, I had better say me, in a case of this kind ; until when the lot fell upon me to do the " nicking " for the party, I went and did it with the most natural air in the world.

There was nothing melodramatic about it either, no stealthy dartings from shadow to shadow with an occasional " hist, I am observed," so dear to the old play-writers. Oh, no. For instance, it once fell to me to " nick " something, and I have the most precise recollection of walking deliberately into a large grocer's shop in Westbourne Grove, its counter laden as usual with samples of goods for sale, and under the nose of the dumfounded salesman, who had watched me enter, lifting a large box of biscuits and retreating before he had even attempted to clear the obstacles between us. And that was only a type of many such adventures. Since, however, this recital tends to become highly immoral, I will only quote one more instance which must even yet linger in the memories of such of its participants as are still alive.

There used to be a large sweet-stuff shop at the corner of Newton Road, Westbourne Grove, which did a fine trade, and was very fully stocked. One night, dared thereunto by some of my companions who had contributed an extraordinary full and varied meal, I entered this shop and calmly lifted a large glass off a side shelf, which contained five or six pounds of chocolate in penny bars covered with silver paper. I took no precautions whatever, beyond leaving the door wide open, nor did I hurry. But upon emerging into the Grove I immediately turned up the dark way of Newton Road, and whistled shrilly for my chums, who were supposed to be keeping *nix*, although their idea of doing so was to get as far away as possible in case of accidents.

I found them all, however, in Kildare Gardens, which used to be reached by a sort of paved alley way guarded by posts at each end, and was a most select, silent, and quasi-aristocratic retreat. A veritable oasis of quiet comfort just off the main artery of Westbourne Grove, then beginning to be famous through the exertions of Mr W. Whiteley. And we sat down on the kerb of the central garden in the dark to divide the spoil. This being done, and each boy's pocket laden with chocolate sticks, one uneasy wight raised the question, " What should we do with the show-glass ? " The obvious thing would have been to leave it there in the dark, but when did boys affect the obvious ?

Then arose the genius of the party and propounded a scheme which made us all cavort with delight (I have said that we were full fed). He proposed that our quartette should advance upon the first house in that utterly silent square, one member carrying the glass container, another the cover, while the other two ascended the steps under the portico and seized, one the knocker, and the other the bell. Then at a given signal the glass must be hurled at the front of the house, the knocker banged, the bell pulled as hard as might be, and—flight. This was at ten p.m.

The instructions were carried out to the foot of the letter ; and never, not in a mutiny on board ship, or a coolie riot, have I heard so infernal a row or seen so sudden an upheaval of temporarily mad people. We four were also suddenly frantic, and in our mad flight up Kildare Terrace, assisted the tumult by snatching at the bells at the garden gates as we ran. But on arriving in the Talbot Road, breathless, we halted, and after a brief consultation, decided that we would return and view the result. We did, and we were completely satisfied. The gardens were full of people, each with a different theory, and the majority clad in strange garb. We circulated and enjoyed ourselves listening. But gradually the concourse melted away; and we, quite happy, stole off to our various lairs.

## CHAPTER III

## FREEDOM AND WANT

FROM the foregoing chapter the reader might hastily arrive at the conclusion that I was certainly qualifying for inclusion in the ranks of criminal classes, since I had arrived at the stages of committing offences against the general peace and well-being without any adequate reason, and had besides no conscience at all, or a conscience void of offence, my only dread being the policeman. I don't know that such a conclusion could be far from the truth, but I would plead that my predatory instincts had been aroused through no fault of my own, and had been fostered by the company into which I was inevitably cast. And then a sudden check was put upon my career, quite by accident, and I shot off at a tangent for a while into an entirely new branch of business.

I met a kind man one day, whose acquaintance I had made about a year previously, quite by accident. I was hungry and despondent, having been unable to find a chance job for nearly two days. He pitied me, and helped me temporarily, but better still offered me employment. He was a billiard-marker, who had just taken a room at a big public-house at Notting Hill, and he wanted a little cheap help such as I could give. So next day I got my first lesson in billiard-marking, and proved, so he said, a very apt pupil, so apt indeed, that by the end of the first evening I could be trusted to mark without fear of my displeasing the players, who, however, were seldom hard to satisfy. And in a week I was as familiar with the whole atmosphere and *argot* of the billiard-room, as if I had been at it all my life.

Doubtless, to the moralist, I should have appeared to be in very great danger, but I can only state what I know to be the fact, that although the talk was almost incessantly of gambling, and a good deal of drinking went on, I heard nothing in the way of language nearly as bad as the women in the laundry used habitually, and I never saw any actual drunkenness. Moreover, since I now always had money in my pocket, being frequently tipped by the players, I had no temptation to pilfer, and became suddenly and entirely honest, in act at any rate, if not from conviction.

And yet by the very irony of fate, I now for the first time fell into the clutches of the law, and was terrified more than I had ever been before. It happened in this way. Among the habitues of the room was a man whom even I knew to be a sharper, a hawk, who preyed upon other men's weaknesses and vices. He usually had some callow youth in training, whom he fleeced until his victim found him out, or had no more money to spend.   He was no welcome visitor, for my employer was a very decent fellow, and hated swindling; but was constrained by the necessities of his position to turn a blind side to much that was shady.

Now our customers seldom came in until the evening, so the afternoon was devoted to cleaning up and getting ready, or attending upon some very rare chance customer.   One day, at about 3 P.M., there were three of us in the room, my employer, the sharper, whom we will call Vivian, and myself.   Vivian was idly knocking the balls about, just killing time, while I was dusting, etc.   Presently my employer said to me, " When Mr Vivian goes, put the cover on, and run down to the —— Hotel, and get the set of balls that the marker will hand you.   You needn't hurry, there will be nothing doing till six o'clock.   I am going out on business, and shall be back at seven."   He then left, and a few minutes after Vivian sauntered out also.

I immediately covered the table, snatched my cap, came out, and locked the room after me.   I did my errand, loitering a good deal on the way, but got back to the house about six.   As soon as I entered the side door, one of the barmen met me, and told me that I was wanted in the bar parlour.   I had never been into that sacred apartment.   Indeed, I hardly knew the landlord or landlady by sight.   But I went, feeling quite trembly, and was at once confronted by my employer, the landlord and landlady, and a keen-looking stranger, whom I instinctively shrank from in dread.

This latter personage at once began to examine me as to my movements since I had left the house, so closely, that I felt more and more afraid, in spite of my perfect innocence, that something was wrong. But the landlady, a handsome, kindly woman, did her best to reassure me, continually speaking comfortable words to me, and giving me a glass of wine. I was gradually losing my fear and becoming indignant at this cross-examination, when the door opened, and in burst another of the frequenters of the house, a professional billiard-player, who had evidently had quite as much drink as was good for him. He burst into the conversation by attacking my tormentor, and expressing decided views as to what he would do to any adjective detective who dared to badger a boy of his. The terrible word detective almost paralysed me with fright. I had always been afraid of a policeman raised to an unknown power, and here I was obviously in the toils of one of that dread fraternity.

However, my warm and injudicious champion was speedily silenced by the cold statement that it was none of his business, because between the hours of 3 and 6 P.M. the landlady's bedroom had been entered and jewellery to the value of £70 had been stolen, and at present there seemed to be no one upon whom suspicion could reasonably rest but me. It was a terrible shock, but though my mouth felt full

c

of dust, and I shivered as if naked to an east wind, I am glad to remember that I sat silent and dry-eyed.

However, there was nothing to be got out of me, and the matter was compromised on the understanding that I was to go on with my work, but on no account to leave the premises under pain of being instantly locked up; and so it came about that for the next four days I lived in luxury, I had a beautiful bed and the best of food, while the barmaids and landlady, all firmly convinced of my innocence, showered caresses and presents on me. Consequently I had no quarrel with my lot, nor did I repine at not being able to go out. As to the suspicion which hung over me, I declare I thought no more about it except when I caught the detective's cold eye upon me, when I shivered involuntarily.

On the fifth day, at about eight in the evening, we were quite busy, when Mr Vivian, whom I had not seen for four days, suddenly walked in. Instantly I recollected that I had forgotten to mention his leaving the room on the fatal day just before I did. Then I was struck by the amazing change in his appearance. He had always before been shabby-genteel, but now the chrysalis had become a butterfly. He wore a glossy new top-hat, a fur-lined coat, open to display a fashionably-cut suit beneath, and patent leather shoes. He smoked a big cigar, and twirled an elaborate cane. With a swagger that compelled attention, he suggested pool and ordered drinks round, and several being willing, a round game began.

Then creeping up to my employer, who appeared as if hypnotised by this gorgeous vision, I whispered my suspicions. Mr T.'s face lighted up, and presently he slipped out of the room, returning with the detective. There was no fuss; at the conclusion of the game the detective invited Mr Vivian outside, and in the result, the affair being fully brought home to him, he was sentenced to a long term of imprisonment. It appeared that when he left the billiard-room on the day in question, he had gone upstairs instead of down, the house being almost deserted, and entering the first room on the next landing which stood open, he had seen the landlady's jewellery lying on the dressing-table, had promptly swept it up, and departed; and he would doubtless have escaped scot-free on account of my stupidity in forgetting about his being there at the time, but for the madness which had prompted him to return and flaunt his fine feathers in his old haunts.

I was considerably petted by all, and the landlady gave me five shillings as well as many kisses. But, alas! only a short time afterwards the house changed hands, and my good friend Mr T. being out of employment, I, too, was once more cast upon my own resources, but this time better off in respect of clothes than I had been for a long time.

I led an extraordinarily nomad life for the next

few weeks, just keeping alive by doing any jobs that came along, but having my few clothes that I had accumulated beyond my immediate wearing safely stored with an old woman, who gave me a shelter when hard pressed, but whom I did not trouble much. And then another acquaintance got me a job on some new buildings that were being erected on the site of an old rookery of tumbledown dwellings, what is now Clanricarde Gardens, Notting Hill. It was an entirely new departure for me, but I was somewhat versatile, and easily acquired the necessary details to enable me to make a show at least at whatever I got a chance to do. My first duty was as time-keeper, and my orders were to allow five minutes' grace to laggards, of whatever class they might be. But here, alas! my conscientious desire to obey my instructions soon made me an object of detestation to everybody on the works except my employer. My book, which I kept with the most rigid justice, was questioned by every delinquent, and I was speedily given to understand that unless I turned a blind eye to the clock, and allowed late comers to pass in without making an entry against them in my book, my life would not only not be worth living, but it was darkly hinted that it would be a very short one.

Then for the first time I learned how devoid of the most elementary principles of justice was the average British workman. Turn a blind eye to his failings and sing loudly his praises, he will laud you to the skies, but only hint that he has his faults, and immediately you are his enemy, to be pursued with relentless ferocity. It was a bitter lesson, but I learned it thoroughly, and I can never forget the faces distorted by passion, and the cruel threats weighted by terrible oaths which were hurled against me on pay day, when " quarters " were stopped on my evidence, merely because I did what I was told.

I only held that position a fortnight, when, yielding to pressure, the boss removed me and made me an assistant to a moulder of ornaments in Roman cement for the fronts of the houses. This was dirty work, but not very hard, and the moulder being an old soldier of the Mutiny time, and garrulous in the extreme about his experiences, I was quite happy. My wages were about eight shillings a week, and the hours from six to six, with an hour and a half for meals, not at all severe. So, upon reflection, I am inclined to think that this was the happiest of all my boyish days ashore, always excluding of course the sheltered time I spent under my aunt's roof.

To my great sorrow this good time came to an end with the finishing of the houses, and I was again adrift. And now let me say in deepest gratitude, that through cold, hunger, wet, and sleeping out, I do not remember ever ailing anything. True, I was stunted in my growth owing to privation, but I was wiry, and except for the curse of bad teeth, I do not think I ever had an ache or pain except the transient ones of cold and hunger. But my great sorrow, continually haunting me, was the fact that I never was able to get permanent employment. No sooner did I seem to get settled and satisfied, than some catastrophe or other would come along and heave me out into unattached desolation again. I was like a homeless dog, ready to fawn upon any possible proprietor, and gladly give up my hated freedom for the certainty of continuous employment.

Now I had heard many things about life at sea, for an uncle of mine, whom I had not seen for years, had commanded ships for a long time, and his remarks upon the sailor's life I had often drank in with greedy care. Nothing that he ever said gave me the slightest desire to adopt his career, for from my earliest recollection I had an analytical mind, and I really had no desire to seek adventure at the cost of all that most people consider makes life worth living. I am afraid my bent was essentially bourgeois, strengthened and set as time wore on and experience came to me. I felt that I could understand, dimly perhaps but certainly, how boys who had never known a hardship, a want unsupplied, should be led away by the glamour of what they read, but how ever a boy who knew what the stress and struggle of life meant ashore could go to sea knowingly, to encounter conditions far worse, I did not understand.

And now, for me at least, the explanation came. It was continuity of employment. You might not like

your job, or your employer might be entirely dis-
satisfied with you, but you were compelled to put up
with each other until the passage was over, at anyrate. This made the prospect of sea-life tolerable
to me. I was under absolutely no apprehensions as
to romantic adventure, for I was certainly not the
stuff of which adventurers are made. All my adventures had been forced upon me, and I was never
so happy as when I was under somebody's command,
if that somebody would only give me an encouraging
word now and then.

So I determined to try and get to sea. But owing
to my puny size I found it very difficult. I was told
that the easiest way to begin was to hang about a
certain public-house in Thames Street, whither
coasting skippers used to resort for their crews. It
was just opposite the Custom-House steps, and was
called the King's Head (or Arms). A certain individual, popularly known as Sam, who was, I
suppose, a species of crimp, was always in evidence and
acted as go-between. To him came all sorts of rough
coasting skippers, masters of barges, of " billy-boys,"
ketches and schooners, in quest of men and boys, and
the latter looked to him as their earthly providence.

How he got paid I do not know, a certain commission from both sides was paid him, I expect. The
candidates were allowed to haunt a grim den, a tap-
room at the back of the public-house, where a good
fire was always blazing, and though dark and gloomy

in the extreme, it afforded a shelter from the bitter blasts which swept down that grimiest of London's business thoroughfares.

I am afraid that it is impossible for me to attempt any adequate description of the time I spent looking for a ship in this terrible place. I had to live, and did, but how I hardly know, for so small an urchin as I stood but little chance in the incessant struggle for employment that went on down there. But I had learned to live upon very little, and it is an incontrovertible fact that the stomach of a young human being that has never known pampering can assimilate food that should, theoretically, derange the digestion of an ostrich. For instance, Fresh Wharf, Thames Street, was the rendezvous of many steamers from Spain, laden with dried fruits, nuts, oranges, etc. In the handling of cases, sacks, and other packages, there was a good deal of breakage, and I could often snatch a few handfuls of currants, nuts, raisins, etc. I always ate of them ravenously, in spite of their copious admixture of dust and dirt, but even after devouring a couple of pounds of currants I never remember feeling the slightest ill effects.

But when by some happy chance I managed to get hold of a few coppers, there was a cook shop opposite the main entrance to Billingsgate Market that never failed to attract me. Their specialité was pea-soup, which was exposed most temptingly in a large tank in one of the windows. It was sold at twopence a

basin ; but the half basin for a penny, not being carefully measured, lacked very little of being full. Moreover, to the initiate, there were degrees in the quality
of this soup. It was freshly made on Monday, and
even then was good. On Tuesday, however, the thick
residue at the bottom of the tank remaining unsold
was left, and the usual ingredients for a fresh mess were
added to it, making it much richer and more substantial. On Wednesday, this process was repeated,
with the result that Wednesday's soup was a thick
pureé in which a spoon would stand erect, and he who
could buy a penn'orth and eat it with a ha'penny hunk
of bread, could go in the strength of that meal for
twenty-four hours without any inconvenience. At
least I can say for myself that I very often did,
and my appetite in those days was terrible, ab-
normal. I really do not seem ever to have been fully
satisfied.

One thing I have reason to be thankful for ; my
pilfering propensities had almost entirely disappeared,
for with the exception of an occasional roll from a
baker's shop, or some unconsidered trifle of cheese or
the dried fruit aforesaid, I never took what was not
mine, and when I did, it was only under the pressure
of great hunger.

Once I made a serious mistake which gave me a
bitter pang, disappointment so keen that I feel the
sting of it even now sometimes. I was ravenously
hungry, and there seemed to be no possibility of getting

anything to eat. So diving down into the shell-fish market beneath the main building of Billingsgate, I watched my opportunity, and filled the breast of my shirt with whelks from a mighty tubful. My booty secured, I hastened back to the gloomy tap-room, there to devour my prize, but was immediately confronted with the difficulty of extracting the whelks from their shells.

I had often seen it done by the men who kept whelk, stalls in the streets, and it looked ridiculously easy. But I could not do it, and I was fain at last to smash the shells, no easy task either. Then clearing the mollusc from débris I tried to eat it, but it was quite impossible, it was tougher than gutta-percha, and I realised that my whelks were unboiled! These morsels require immense masticatory powers to deal with them at any time, but uncooked they would defy the jaws of a stone-crusher.

So time passed, oh so slowly, and although I made frequent appeals to Sam, he always looked at me indulgently, and told me to wait a bit. And every day I saw men and boys being shipped, and practising the recognised ritual, by virtue of which they were permitted to use the public-house as a house of call. This consisted of receiving from the skipper engaging them a shilling for handsel money, which coin was always spent in two pots of beer and two screws of shag, which was shared by all the waiting ones. It was of no use to me, for I neither drank beer or smoked tobacco, but although I would have been glad to take my share in coin, if only a ha'penny, that was not to be thought of.

One adventure befell me about this time, which left a most vivid impression on me. Among the fellows who hung about looking to Sam for a ship would be occasionally a big boy warmly clad in coarse nautical clothing, and an indefinable air about him of being under some invisible supervision. One of these fellows became quite friendly with me, and at last in a burst of confidence informed me that he had been in prison for some minor offence, and that by the bounty of the authorities he had been clothed as I saw him, and every night a shilling was given to him for his maintenance while looking for a ship, which he was sure to get before long, because Sam had special instructions on his behalf.

One night my new found friend informed me that he was going to sea the next day, and invited me to share his hospitality, with the special inducement that I should be introduced to his sweetheart. I accepted with grateful alacrity, and soon after dark I accompanied him to the purlieus of Spitalfields to a rag-and-bottle shop kept by his inamorata's father. The shop was frowsty and mildewy as these places must be, and the old man might well have served Dickens as a model for Krook, but he was very affable, and his buxom slatternly daughter was obviously much in love with my companion. At any rate a feast of fried fish and potatoes and bread were spread for us, and although our surroundings savoured of the charnel-house, and the only light was from a tallow dip in a ginger-beer bottle, I fully enjoyed my meal, not that I got enough, but the razor edge was certainly taken off my hunger.

After we had eaten, the old man sent me out for a quartern of gin, which was diluted with hot water and sugar, and shared by the three—I had some drink from the tap. Then the old merchant engaged my attention with some, to me, absolutely unintelligible conversation, while his daughter and her young man, seated upon a pile of mixed coloured (rags), made ostentatious love to each other. It was all very uninteresting to me, and I was growing weary of it, when at last Jem, my friend, rose, and bidding his host and sweetheart good-night bade me follow him.

I went unquestioningly, he regaling me all the way with descriptions of the great career which lay before him when he should marry Jemima, and succeed to the old man's business—which to him apparently contained the potentialities of wealth beyond the dreams of avarice. But, oh the weary trudge! I was ready to drop where I stood, when he turned and went into a lodging-house in one of the slums of Westminster, paying threepence each for us at a little office at the door. Thence we passed into a large room with plain benches and tables, at which sat a large number of rough-looking men, none of whom however took any notice of us. There was an immense kitchen range at one side of this room, with a splendid fire blazing, and at the sides a number of kettles, frying-pans, and gridirons.

My companion then gave me sixpence and sent me out marketing. I bought a ha'porth of tea and sugar (mixed), a farthing's worth of milk, a penn'orth of butter, half a loaf (twopence), and two fine bloaters for three halfpence, returning with my load and three farthings change. We had a wash, made our tea, and thoroughly enjoyed an ample meal in comfort, after which, so sleepy was I, that I could hardly sit up, though I endeavoured to read an old newspaper. I had just whispered a query to Jem as to whether I couldn't get to bed, when the door-keeper came in and beckoned me, retreating at the same time towards the door. I followed him, and when we reached his office he silently placed three pennies in my hand, then said, " Get out o' this." I looked appealingly, questioningly at him, but his stern face and pointed finger did not invite delay, so I slunk out into the night and down to St James's Park, where, climbing over the railings, I found a quiet spot in a shrubbery, and laid me down to sleep ; a little shivery, but quite easy in my mind.

# CHAPTER IV

## MY TRADE APPRENTICESHIP
## FINISHES

UNDOUBTEDLY there was a good deal of mystery about the proceedings which closed the last chapter, but I was in those days very little concerned with causes, I had enough trouble with results. So I did not try to speculate, only feeling glad that my friend was evidently all right. And after all I had spent a very pleasant evening, my belly was nearly full, and I was threepence to the good. So why worry, more especially as it was certain that any attempt at investigation on my part could only lead to trouble for me, and I was ever anxious to avoid trouble of any kind.

In the course of the day I drifted down to the King's Arms again, but saw nothing of my friend. So towards evening, I made bold to ask Sam if he had seen · him, and received the reply that he had sailed that morning in a schooner for Spain. I have never seen him since, but I have not been able to forget him.

One never-failing source of amusement I had during this long weary time, for even if hungry and cold young things will try to play, was in the Tower of London, into which I often dodged past the guards. I was often caught and driven back, but that only whetted my appetite for getting in.  In my numerous visits I explored many portions of the old building that visitors never see, and I had many a good meal given me by the kind-hearted mess-cooks of the garrison.  And by stealthily joining myself on to parties of visitors, I went the rounds of all the show-places, into which entrance in those days could only be had by payment, and was mightily amused at hearing the same old story told with hardly an altered word by the " beef-eaters."

I have mentioned this particularly, because opportunities for play in that stern and dingy quarter of London were very few, and when I got out of Thames Street for a brief space into the cloister-like atmosphere of the Tower, I really did feel as if I was in another world, and I never quite got rid of that eerie feeling when I was alone in some unfrequented corner, that I was moving among a crowd of ghosts, who in the past had suffered and died within those grim walls. One night I found myself belated in the horse armoury, and as I could not find my way out, and dared not call, for that I knew I had no business there, I curled myself up in a snug corner and went to sleep, awaking in the morning with the sun streaming into my eyes, and with a firm determination to run no such risk again.  I got in there by climbing over a big gate with a cheval-de-frise on the top, and I got out the same way without being observed. I suppose if I had been caught my punishment would have been something mediæval, for the crime was, to say the least of it, unusual.

And now the grim fact began to thrust itself upon me without possibility of mistake that it was hopeless ever to expect to get a ship by doing as I was doing. The vessels that got their crews in this way were all pitifully undermanned, and consequently whoever was chosen for employment in one of them must of necessity be strong and inured to hard work. Indeed, this choice was carried so far, that the skippers invariably felt the hands of the candidates, and if they were not calloused like the skin of a yam, the defect was fatal, supposing that there was any competition. My hands were only felt once, and that more I suspect as a matter of form, for nothing came of it.

At last I asked Sam timidly if he really thought I stood any chance of getting a ship there. He looked down at me as if he had just seen me for the first time, pondered a moment (but about nothing I am sure), then suddenly remembering my question, said, "Oh no, not till you've a-growed a bit. You better stow-away." I said, "Thank you, sir," and moved off fully determined, whatever happened, not to stow-away. Going to sea, I thought, was bad enough in any case, but from what I had heard stowaways stood a good chance of getting first a good hammering, then a tremendous lot of hard work, and very little food, and prison at the journey's end.   It was a programme that did not appeal to me.

Nevertheless, it was with a sinking heart that I turned away from Thames Street that night.   I felt that I could not hold my own in the rough and tumble life of the streets much longer, and I craved with all my heart and soul for a master.   I know that there are boys who, even in good homes, have the nomad instinct so strongly implanted that they cannot be contented anywhere, will endure, nay, embrace voluntarily all kinds of privation, so long as they may vagabondise, but I was not one of them.   My early training was all against it.   I longed for a home, and to have some one in authority over me, although I could not help admitting to myself that I had not made the best of my chances, such as they were.

But as the darkest hour is just before the dawn according to the adage, so when my prospects of getting to sea were at what appeared to be the lowest ebb, I suddenly bethought me of the possibility of finding my uncle, whom I have before alluded to as being master of a ship.   More by accident than design, I discovered him, and although he was evidently not overjoyed to see me he agreed to take me to sea with him at the wage of five shillings per month.

Of my early experiences at sea, I have told at length in the " Log of a Sea Waif," and therefore I cannot repeat them here.   I can only point out that there

D

seemed to be a fatality about the matter, something working against my becoming a seafarer, since I was shipwrecked on my first voyage and landed in Havana, where, because of the old trouble, my puny size, I could not get a ship, and consequently I returned to one of my old employments, namely, that of billiard-marker. It was at the Hotel St Isabel in the Plaza de Armas, and here for some months I led a very happy if entirely demoralising life for one so young. I received no wages, but the best of food and lodging, and the tips given me by the frequenters of the billiard-room were so many that I always had plenty of money.

But strangely enough, although I certainly ought to have known the value of money from my previous training, now being provided liberally with all I needed, I made no attempt to save, but distributed my wealth among the sailors at the port, with whom I always forgathered when not on duty. Thus it came about that when I was one day taken charge of by the Consul again, and after he had scolded and threatened me for some time, because, as he said, I had dared to remove myself from his care without his permission, I was entirely penniless.

He put me on board a vessel bound for home via Mobile, Alabama, and when I reached Liverpool I was not merely penniless, I was almost naked, and it was winter. I had no claim upon anybody for wages, no knowledge of where to go, and I felt as if the fates had indeed been unkind to me. But I found a good

Samaritan in the guise of a poor woman, who kept a small eating-house, and she took me in and allowed me to work for my keep. And thus I added one more to my smattering of trades, that of waiter; the maid-of-all-work part I was very well versed in. It was all the kinder of her, because the business was hardly substantial enough to support even the slight additional burden which I placed upon it. Our principal trade was with the poverty-stricken dock-labourers, whose orders were usually for a basin of broth at a penny and a ha'porth of bread, except when flush, they were able to treat themselves to a twopenny plate of potato-pie. Everybody seemed to be bitterly poor, and it was little wonder to me that when a sailor just paid off did happen to come in and show the gleam of gold, eyes grew wolfish and fingers involuntary crooked themselves.

I had not been there more than a couple of months, when my mistress gave me clearly to understand that I must be off, for she could not support me any longer; although God knows I did work hard for every mouthful I ate (and I was never stinted). Then chance threw in my way an opportunity of trying yet another trade, that of carver of ornamental wood work for ship decoration. The workshop was next door, and I had made the proprietor's acquaintance through running in there occasionally for chips. But I do not think I should ever have dreamed of asking him for employment, if my mistress had not one day, when in conversation with him, mentioned that she was going to start me off. In the goodness of his heart he offered me employment, and I leaped at the offer. I started work the very next morning, for my keep, though what he paid my late mistress I never knew. I was an apt pupil, and he was very kind, so that I soon became quite useful to him. I learned to sharpen the multitude of tools he used, and also to rough out with mallet and chisel the carvings that he and his brother finished off.

It was congenial and pleasant work, and I felt as if at last I had found my groove, and that I was destined to be a wood-carver. But alas my evil genius was on my track. I pleased my employer too well. So well indeed, that his brother, older than he, but a journeyman under him, became violently jealous of me, and lost no opportunity of showing his dislike. That, however, did not trouble me much, except when my boss was away, which was seldom, because under his benevolent eye I was entirely happy and stimulated to do my very best. Even at this great lapse of time I remember with a glow at my heart, how gently he reproved me for the mistakes I made, how warmly he praised me whenever I was able to do exactly what he wished me to do, and I have no recollection whatever of his ever being harsh, unjust, or even inconsiderate.

He had many odd jobs of repairing to do, the ornamental work on ship's bows and sterns was always getting knocked away when coming into or going out of dock ;

and generally it had to be repaired *in situ*, only the worst damage being worked over in the shop and then taken down and fitted on. There was something to me very delightful in sitting alongside him on a precarious-looking stage overhanging the black water in a dock, listening to his cheery remarks, his clear tenor as he sang snatches of song, or his whistle, melodious as a skylark's. He never seemed to be weary or discouraged, or ill-tempered ; and I know that I rendered him all the loving homage of which I was capable.

It was often bitterly cold as we swang on our stages in those exposed positions, but it never seemed to affect him, his blows with the chisel upon the intricate design before him never seemed to vary their certitude or his patience, to falter, even when a cross-grained piece of wood did fly and spoil the pattern. And then how delightful at meal times, when we were too far from home to go thither for food, to accompany him to some cosy cook-shop, and eat with him, treated just as his son, I was going to say, only unhappily I know that he treated me far far better than many fathers treat their sons.

Unfortunately as the time went on it became increasingly evident that this present happiness of mine was drawing rapidly near its end. The brother of whom I spoke was a most morose and sullen man, a very poor workman, who could never be trusted to do a job properly, not I should say lazy, but incapable of doing good work, and fully conscious of the fact.   He would not have earned his salt anywhere, but his good brother kept him on out of charity. Now my presence there annoyed him, and whenever I was left alone with him he used to give me a very bad time.   And when his brother returned he always made an evil report of my behaviour, but I had the satisfaction of feeling that he was not believed, as indeed he did not deserve to be.

At last, however, the matter culminated in this way.   The boss was working upon one of the African boats, and had left me with his brother to do some cross-cut sawing.   Now every one should know that this is heavy work even for practised men, and when a boy of thirteen and a man of thirty are working together, the man ought to remember the disparity between their ages and strength.   But this only gave my small-witted enemy his opportunity, and when I had perforce to stop from fatigue he burst into a flood of sarcastic swearing.   When he paused for breath, I made some injudicious reply, and was immediately sent flying across the shop by a blow on the side of the head.   Smarting with pain I snatched up a mallet, and flung it at the coward with all my strength, and I am glad to say it landed on his nose, even though my successful shot was productive of much serious trouble for me.

Then I bolted from the place, for I feared that he would kill me, as indeed I daresay he would have done had I remained. That evening my good friend came into the cook-shop, and found me sitting white and trembling, waiting for him. He was as usual very kind, though he reproved me gravely for having broken his brother's nose. But when he asked me if I wasn't sorry for having done it, I gladly remember that I truthfully told him no. A ghost of a smile gathered around his mouth, but shaking his head he went on to say, "I'm terribly sorry to part with you, Tommy, for I had got very fond of you, but I've got to choose between you and my brother, and I can't turn him off. He swears he will murder you when he sees you, so you'll have to go. Poor little boy, I do hope you'll get something else soon." And with that he pressed half a sovereign into my hand, and went away.

I need not enlarge upon the fact of its being a terrible blow to me, nor apologise for shedding a good many hot tears after he was gone, because he was the first person during my independent career who had satisfied my burning desire to be loved. I felt that he was fond of me, and knew that his lightest word of commendation was more precious to me than any treasure would have been. I glory in the knowledge that he never once had to scold me for anything but mistakes. I did try with all my heart and soul to please him, because I loved him, and now I had lost him. And the wide world before me again looked very unsympathetic and dreary.

Somehow Liverpool seemed very distasteful to me.

My weary wanderings around the docks, and the
continual unsuccess I had met with in looking for a
ship, had made me feel as if I might possibly do better
in my own big village, and I realised that I now
possessed the means of getting back to it again. So
the next morning I bade farewell to Mrs Dickey, my
landlady, who was quite unmoved at the parting, for
she was very angry with me for getting the sack, as she
termed it, and toddled off to Lime Street, where I had
no difficulty whatever in getting a half ticket to London,
nor felt troubled because after paying for it I had only
1s. 7½d. left out of my precious half-sovereign.

I must not omit to mention that Mrs Dickey gave
me a big hunk of bread and cheese when I told her
that I was going to London, but she did not give me
a kiss, which I should have prized far more, for I was
an affectionate little chap, and was starving for love.
But, poor woman, she was heavily burdened, and no
doubt was heartily glad to get rid of me, although I
cannot think that she had ever been out of pocket by
me, for I certainly earned my keep. Still she did not
want me, so there is no more to be said.

It was a glorious spring day, and the novelty of my
first long train journey made me forget all my troubles.
Moreover, I felt full of importance to think that I was
a passenger by that great train. Every inch of that
journey was full of interest to me. I had a seat by the
window, and my eyes fairly ached with the intensity
of my gaze out over the beautiful country of which,

until then, I had seen practically nothing. I remember that I spoke to no one, and no one spoke to me, though several of my fellow-passengers must have wondered who or what was the ill-clad urchin who sat so quietly and gazed so intently at the flying landscape.

I was quite sorry when the train arrived at Euston, and I had to march out into the mean net-work of streets which surround the badly situated station, for now I began to wonder what I should do in the vast city which was my birth-place, but in which I had no friends or abiding-corner. It was all so familiar, and yet so inhospitable. Had I only known where to look, there were many places where I could have found shelter and help, but for lack of that useful knowledge, how many wanderers like myself have died?

One thing I felt certain of, which was that I could not now take my place among the ranks of my former companions, I could not compete with them for sale of papers, or the numerous odd jobs that boys can do. For one thing I had never been much of a pusher—I was always more ready to stand aside than to press forward in the race for a job, though willing enough to take one if I got the chance—and for another, I had lost the sense of familiarity with those conditions of life ashore, while the new experience I had gained was here of no use to me.

Therefore I made no effort in this direction, but after wandering aimlessly about until I was dog tired, I went down the West India Dock Road until I came to a house with the legend painted up—" Seamen's Boarding House," and knocked at its door with my heart thumping furiously. A terrible looking man with a great grizzled beard and a voice like a foghorn came to the door and looked at me in silence. I swallowed nothing once or twice, then taking out my discharge from my last ship, which I had treasured as if it were a bank-note for a hundred pounds, I said, " Please, Sir, may I stay here. I want a ship and I've got a good discharge. I'll pay you out of my advance if you'll get me a ship." He growled.

" Wher's yer dunnage (clothes) ? I answered faintly, " I've got none, I was shipwrecked." He hesitated for a moment, then rumbled, " come inside," and with my heart leaping, I went into a stuffy front parlour, where sat two or three men, obviously ill at ease, and a fat pale faced woman who was looking fixedly in the fire. Taking me by the shoulder, the boarding-master led me up to the woman saying—

" Here, mother, here's an able seaman wants to stop here. He's got no clothes and no money, but he says he'll pay me out of his advance note."

Then I saw with a wave of pity that she was blind. She turned at the voice and put out both hands, touching me and feeling me from my forehead down to my waist.

" Why, Bill," she cried, " its only a child, a poor little boy," and with a motherly movement she drew me to her, and felt me all over again. Then she asked me many questions, all of which I answered with absolute truth, for there could be no reason why I should not. And at the conclusion of her examination I was entered on the books of the house as a boarder, while the master went growling about saying that at this rate he would soon be in the workhouse. But the old lady kept me by her side and whispered that it was only Mr Jones's fun, he didn't mean anything by it, and that he would surely do his best to get me a ship soon.

This was true, for though he was always grumpy, and given to regaling his boarders at meal times with lugubrious forebodings of his speedy entrance to Poplar Workhouse, with victuals at the price they were and so many hungry outward-bounders to feed, I know he did his best for me ; did it so well, that in five days from entering his house I obtained a ship as boy with a wage of twenty-five shillings per month, to my intense surprise. I received, like the rest of the crew, a note for a month's advance, which I handed over to him at once. Out of this he gave me a small supply of most necessary clothes bought second hand, so that he must have dealt with me not merely honestly but in a spirit of generosity.

And now I come to the close of my shore apprenticeship, as it may be termed, for although I had a very severe time upon my return to Liverpool from that voyage (again shipwrecked), I never again but once had a job ashore until I left the sea as a profession finally. That time I spent upon a farm in New Zealand, and although it certainly had its comic side, I was such an utterly complete failure at it that I blush now when I think of the figure I made. Fortunately it did not last long, about two months, and in spite of my colossal ineptitude I really think I earned all that I received, which was my keep and a pair of boots.

Not indeed that I could have claimed to have been a shining success in any of the various commercial paths wherein I had strayed, more or less painfully, but I must plead that I was very young, and entirely without the guidance which youngsters have a right to expect from their elders. And now I must make a jump of a great many years, to the time in fact when relentless need drove me into commercialism again. And with this what I suppose I must call the serious part of my narrative begins.

# CHAPTER V

## INTO TRADE IN SPITE OF MYSELF

SPLENDID and universal as are the attainments of seamen, it is only the bare truth to say that one of the rarest qualifications to find among them is commercial aptitude. There are, of course, notable exceptions, and in the days when masters and officers of vessels were allowed to add to their income substantially by trade with the natives of the countries which they visited, and were granted a certain amount of space in the hold wherein to store the merchandise they bought, the trading instinct must have been fairly general. Indeed there are not wanting cynics at sea to-day, who will tell you that what with the slop-chest, tobacco selling, and the outrageous rates of exchange, many a deep water skipper of a sailing ship could give points to an Armenian. And the latter is supposed by sailors to be equal in, let us call it trading power, to five Parsees, one of whom again equals five Jews.

But I do not think this is fair. It does not follow that a man is a born trader because he can sell necessaries to people who must have them from him or go without, and cannot go without. It only argues lack of conscience on the part of the seller. And to expect, without lack of competition, the same characteristics would, I am afraid, be indicative of a weak mind. At any rate I am quite certain that, speaking generally, a sailor when he comes ashore is helpless in the hands of business people, and that it is a very long while before he is able to think their thoughts and walk in their ways.

So when I first settled down ashore to steady employment in an office at a fixed salary of £2 per week, after fifteen years of irresponsibility as regards domestic affairs, I quickly learned that I was very callow indeed in those matters. My first false step was in buying furniture, wherewith to make a home, on the hire system. It must be remembered that I had a wife and one child, but that I was practically beginning a new life. And I did so by hanging round my neck a burden of debt which I did not get rid of for fifteen years, and then—but I must not anticipate the regular sequence of my story.

The next was to take a house. I had tried apartments several times, but something always went wrong, I was always made to feel that I was only in the house on sufferance, and being an enthusiast for peace, I always moved rather than have a row. But moving as a fairly regular experience is apt to pall upon one. It costs a good deal of money even when you hire the local greengrocer's van and horse

at one and sixpence an hour, and it is very hard work,
for unless you buckle to and do the lion's share yourself, you find at nightfall that you have just got in,
you have parted with the bulk of your savings, and
the best part of a heavy night's work is before you,
putting up bedsteads and reducing the chaotic heap
of your belongings to a condition in which you can
find what you want within reasonable distance of
the time that you want it.

For this and other reasons which I need not now
specify I decided to take a house. I satisfied myself
that by letting the floor below and the floor above the
one I intended to keep for ourselves at the current
rate in the neighbourhood, carefully ascertained
beforehand, that I should live rent free or nearly so,
and of course in a neighbourhood like that it was
unthinkable that I should ever be empty. I mean
the house of course. By which process of reasoning
I demonstrated that I possessed one of the prime
requirements of a tradesman—hope that my venture
would be justified by the profit on my outlay.

But, alas, I was not made of the fibre necessary in
order to be a successful sub-landlord. By the end
of the first year of my tenancy I had come to the conclusion that I was a known mark for all the undesirables
in the neighbourhood. If a tenant was clean he was
utterly unreasonable, looking upon me as his bond-
slave, and his right to do as he liked indefeasible, even
though it might be destructive to my peace of mind

or rest of body. And his one argument in reply to any remonstrance was, "I pay my rent and can go where I like. And don't you interfere with me."

Amiable tenants found excuses for non-payment of rent or were dirty. One I remember brought a sofa into the house the stuffing of which I think must have been mainly bugs. I learned of this by the house becoming infested beyond belief, and seeing hordes of these odoriferous insects coming downstairs. This led to my making enquiries, when the origin or hot-bed was found to be the sofa aforesaid. Nothing could have been more amiable than the manner in which my mild remonstrances were received or more suave than the manner in which my modest request for a small contribution towards the heavy expense of getting the house cleansed and fumigated was denied.

Other lodgers smilingly avowed their inability to pay their rent, and playfully urged me to get it if I could. Others fought furious battles overhead, or engaged in gymnastic exercises which brought the ceilings down, or contracted an offensive and defensive alliance with each other (the top and bottom floors), with the avowed object of making us "sit up," in which I may add they were surprisingly successful.

I do not say that I never had a desirable or satisfactory tenant, because I had several, but alas, I never had two sets of desirable tenants at the same time. And one of the nicest families I ever let my ground floor to, seven in number, developed scarlet fever and gave me perhaps more anxiety and put me to more expense than all the rest put together.   Taking them all round though, I can see there was ample copy among them for a book on queer tenants.   There were the widow and her two daughters, aged respecttively seventeen and fourteen.   The latter used to take turn about to beat their mother, and the screams would at once attract a crowd, for it was a populous street.   Then when I interfered, the whole three would turn upon me, the mother fiercest of all, and threaten me with unheard of penalties for daring to interfere with their *menus plaisirs*.   There was a fine specimen of a British working man, who for six days of the week was a credit to his country ; clean, punctual, honest, and hard working.   But on Saturday night he invariably got partially drunk, and after eleven P.M. amused himself until about 1 A.M. by stamping heavily up and down stairs, along the passage, past my door, out of the front door, slamming it behind him with great violence, immediately re-entering and repeating the performance, and all the time uttering the most bloodthirsty and blasphemous threats against me.   Me ! who never exchanged a word with him, and against whom I could have had no possible ground of complaint, except perhaps that he, being a socialist of the Keir Hardie or Will Crooks type, was bound to show his resentment for having to pay me rent.

E

But I must not multiply instances, though the temptation to do so is very great, but pass on to what must have appeared to the reader to be the inevitable result.  I got behind with *my* rent.  Worry began to prey upon me, to gnaw my vitals, and make me look almost despairingly around for some means of earning more money.  Fortunately for me, my landlord was a kind hearted tradesman, who had a splendid business of his own, and who had invested some of the profits in this house which I rented.  I paid my rent direct to him, and always met with the most kindly consideration short of letting me off paying altogether, which I could not expect.

Unhappily, however, his kindness led to the inevitable result.  He became my last resource.  Creditors who would not wait got paid while he continued to wait.  Finding that he would take excuses and grant delays which no one else would, I grew to depend upon him, and what was worse, to feel aggrieved because others were not like-minded.  It is a vicious circle in which an enormous number of people travel, but I think it will be found that the majority of them are too soft-hearted to insist upon their own dues being paid them promptly, and are always filled with wonder that their creditors are not actuated by the same benevolent sentiments.

Meanwhile, if the charge of unbusiness-like and soft-hearted habits could justly have been laid to my charge, extravagance certainly could not.  I lived personally poorer than any day labourer, scarcely ever tasting meat except on Sunday, and then only the cheapest and coarsest parts of the animal, which my skill in cookery rendered palatable in stews and curries to all of us. I walked to and fro to business—a matter of ten miles—daily, and never spent a penny for anything but absolute necessaries. My sole recreation was in open air meetings for religious purposes, which to me were theatre, circus, and concert all in one. Yet I grew steadily poorer, and as to saving, well, the only possible means of doing that was by insuring my life, which I am glad to say I did to the amount of ten shillings a month, the utmost I could spare.

I only mention these few details to show how I was being steadily thrust in the direction of doing something outside my regular office work, something to utilise the time which I felt was being wasted. My long sea-training had made me an early riser, indeed I could get up cheerfully at any time (and can still), and nothing was more irksome to me than lying abed after my body was satisfied with rest. I used to get up at most unearthly hours in the summer and go long walks with a book, and lie and read after I came home at night until I could see no more. Yet, thank God, I am writing this in a minute hand at the age of fifty, without spectacles or feeling the need of them.

Constantly the thought would intrude itself, " why can't I get something to do during the hours I am free from the office and don't want to sleep ? " My fellow-clerks, with but very few exceptions, had outside employment, but this was usually literary, and for that I felt I had neither aptitude nor training. Mechanical bent I felt sure I had none, for I could hardly drive a nail or put a screw in without spoiling the head. In short, I felt that I was a drug in the market, a passable seaman perhaps, but I had thrown that employment behind me for ever, and now I was a very mediocre *junior* clerk, getting on into middle age and being reminded of my deficiencies—which, alas, I knew only too well—every day by my superiors.

Since these are confessions, shall I be blamed for saying that I prayed for extra work ? Well, anyhow I did ; prayed as fervently as some people do at certain crises for forgiveness of sin. You all know that I was what is called very religious, that is to say, I lived an exceedingly narrow life, looking upon all amusements as snares of the devil, and consoled myself continually, for the loss of all that my fellows seemed to prize in this world, by the thought of the glories of immortality. Happily, I did not condemn all who differed from me in my theological concepts to an eternity of unmentionable agony, because although this was insisted upon as a cardinal item in their belief by the people with whom I associated, my heart or brain or feelings—or my thinking gear—simply would not let me do so. In fact, I felt that such an idea of the God I believed in was blasphemy. And my freely expressed opinions led to my being excommunicated in due form from several bodies of Christians with whom I worked.

Yes, I did pray for some means of earning a little extra money, but at the same time I was acutely conscious of my lack of ability to do anything that employers of overtime men had any use for. Anything in the way of manual labour was of course out of the question, while as to canvassing ! With shame I confess that I did try one or two of the specious advertisements in the daily papers, which promise so much and perform so little. But I speedily found that at soliciting custom from door to door I should starve. I was too sensitive. So far from realising the ideal of never taking no for an answer, which was always held up to me, a glum look, or a door slammed in my face, was enough to put me off my business for a whole evening. I realised then, as I had never done before, the terrible truth of Longfellow's lines, long as they had been graven in my heart—

> " Who amid their wants and woes,
> Hear the sound of doors that close,
> And of feet that pass them by.
> Grown familiar with disfavour,
> Grown familiar with the savour
> Of the bread by which men die ! "
>                                         " The Legend Beautiful. '

But I realised also that whatever my sentimental feelings on the matter might be, the need of earning something extra grew not merely none the less, but ever more pressing. Yet nothing seemed to present itself, nor were there any of my acquaintances able to throw anything at all in my way. At last a small chance came, a curious little eddy in one of the backwaters of life, and I, ready for anything that I could do, seized it. A friend of mine used to add to his income by selling to his fellow-clerks such small articles of jewellery or fancy goods as he could obtain at wholesale price, taking payment for them weekly or monthly as the case might be. He was also Agent for several other concerns such as Insurance Companies, photographers, etc., and finally finding that he had more on his hands than he was able to do, and attend to his clerical work as well, he decided to give up that part of his outside work that was least profitable and imposed the greatest amount of extra work upon him. This was the fancy goods business.

This he offered to me with his connection both for buying and selling, and full explanation as to profits, etc. He did not certainly go so far as to supply the capital, but he did everything else that he could in order that I might start fair. Given a small amount of capital, the business was simple enough. Having once obtained the entrée to certain large wholesale firms in Houndsditch and its neighbourhood, anything comprised within the enormous range of articles known as " fancy " could be purchased for cash at wholesale prices, even in one twelfth of a dozen, or " one only " as the trade term goes. And often an article from a " clearing line," or goods which have been in stock longer than they ought to have been, and were clamouring to be dispersed, could be purchased for a sum which certainly did not represent the cost of the raw material of the manufacture, to say nothing of the skilled workmanship lavished upon it.

Goods were never bought on speculation, my capital would not admit of that; indeed I often borrowed a few shillings for the purpose of buying an ordered article, so that I was almost completely debarred from taking advantage of these "clearing line" opportunities. No, I bought when I had an order say for £1. I delivered the article and accepted three sums of ten shillings each on successive monthly pay days. Now, at first blush and remembering that I took no risk, this may seem an exorbitant profit, but I found in practice that it was not so, and that many retail establishments where goods are sold for cash charge quite as much for similar goods as I did. Still, I am not apologising, I am merely stating facts.

I did a strictly limited and non-expanding business for many reasons, but principally because although I developed a fine business aptitude as far as the mere buying and selling went, I had no notion of accumulating a little capital—there were so many crying needs to be supplied at home that I could not turn a deaf ear to them when I had a little money made out of office hours like this, and assume that I had not got it at all. Also, because I dared not incur any risks, my customers had to be confined to those of my acquaintances whose affairs were almost as well known to me as my own.

But timid and tentative as these little excursions of mine into trade were, they were laden with instruction and interest; yes, and occasionally a fair amount of amusement was obtained also. For instance, most of the wholesale dealers whom I patronised were Hebrews, and I, having like all sailors associated Jews generally with the distinctively evil types of the ancient race who flourish in sailor towns as tailors and boarding masters, was at first inclined to be very shy and cautious in my dealings with them. Before long, however, I made two curious discoveries. One was that the Jews whom I now met in business were kindly, straightforward, honest, and hospitable, in fact quite unlike my preconceived notions of Jews. The other was perhaps a partial explanation of the former—wherever I went among them I was taken for a Jew myself! At first my silly prejudices led me rather to resent this; but I have always felt proud of an open mind, and after considering the matter carefully, I came to the conclusion that the mistake was rather a compliment than otherwise.

Now, as far as I know or can ascertain, the records of the old Dorset family from which I am descended contain no reference to any admixture of Jewish blood, and so although I am a firm believer in transmitted physical and mental characteristics, I am com-

pelled to believe that this Hebraic cast of features
is either accidental or is a throw back to some remote
ancestor.   Be that as it may, I reaped a very definite
benefit from my Jewish physiognomy, in that I had
never any difficulty in getting my tiny orders filled
at any Jewish wholesale house, and if one firm could
not supply me I was at once passed on to another
who could.   Here also I may pause for a moment
to point out, that during my recent visit to Australia
and New Zealand, I was always sought after and made
much of by the Jewish community, which is very
highly respected and powerful in those distant colonies.
And when I laughingly used to disclaim any tribal
connection they invariably assured me that it really
did not matter, because even if I was a true Goy or
Gentile, I had so many traits in common with the
best of Israel that I might well be accepted as one of
the Sephardim.

Well, this digression is merely to show how, in those
feeble attempts at trade, I was curiously helped and
interested in this strange by-way.   But undoubtedly
had I been a true son of Israel I should have become
a successful merchant, for I had every encouragement
to launch out except capital—and I now think that
even that essential might have been forthcoming had I
chosen to seek it.   I did not, but contented myself
with endeavouring to fill such small orders for bags,
workboxes, christening sets, clocks, cheap watches
and chains, etc., as came my way, gaining in the process

a great amount of insight into the workings of business of a certain kind.

One curious discovery I made which was of great service to me on several occasions. (I hope the term " great " will be understood as relative to my small affairs, in which shillings loomed as important as hundreds of pounds to some people, and where a penny tram or bus ride often meant a considerable shortage in a meal.) Of course I was not very long ashore before I became familiar with the working of the poor man's bank, the much abused pawnbroker. Many a time in dire distress through sickness or some other sudden strain I have blessed the means whereby a temporary loan could be effected without straining the resources of a friend, or risking a rebuff from some one I thought friendly. It is commonly supposed among people comfortably off that only drunkards and shiftless people support pawnbrokers. Ah, well, a great many other suppositions of a similar kind are made by those who do not know, but I can assure them that were it not for the pawnbroker pauperism would be much greater than it is.

I go farther and declare that it preserves the borrower's self-respect, in that he need not cringe to those who may be temporarily better off than he is, as long as he has any portable property that a pawn-broker will look at, while the possession of such articles proves that he has had foresight and been thrifty when it was possible for him to be so. Better means might doubtless be devised for the assistance of the temporarily embarrassed worker without robbing him of his self-respect, but until they are, it is cruel as well as foolish to slander the pawnbroker.

And now for the curious discovery. On one occasion I had purchased a watch and chain for a customer, and had borrowed some money to make up what I lacked of the price of the articles. My customer had a misfortune which prevented him from keeping his bargain, and in consequence I was left with the goods on my hands, and no means of repaying the loan. In my extremity I turned to a pawnbroker of my acquaintance and asked him to lend me as much as he could upon the watch and chain. He asked me if I was likely to redeem them, and I frankly answered no. Thereupon he lent me within a couple of shillings of the price I had paid for them, and as I soon afterwards sold the ticket for five shillings, I made a small profit on the transaction.

But this side line I could not feel was legitimate trade, and so, although I was several times driven to avail myself of this knowledge to meet a sudden emergency, I never attempted to use it except when compelled. Another thing, I was never tempted, as I have known traders to be, to pawn goods which, being unpaid for, were really not my own. This was because I had no credit from anyone except from the landlord and the Furnishing Company, and I found that burden heavy enough in all conscience. But I have known a woman working for a wholesale mantle house, and employing a dozen other women, to make up goods and pawn them to pay her workers, take a portion of the order in and get more material out, and so on in a vicious circle, with what wear and tear of mental and moral fibre no one could possibly guess. No wonder the lunacy rate rises.

And yet when you come to think of it, there is only a quantitative, not a qualitative difference between that poor hunger-bitten woman making ulsters at sixpence each, and some of our motor-driving fur-coated manipulators of stocks and shares who pawn one lot of somebody else's shares to buy a lot for a third party, and pledge the latest purchase to redeem or contango or bedevil something else. Yes, there is one great difference, the stock-dealer neither goes hungry nor cold, nor runs much risk of " doing time," because he happens to be caught with ten shillings short at delivery time.

# CHAPTER VI

## DEVELOPMENTS

THE appetite grows by what it feeds upon, says the proverb, and this is indubitably true of extra work. No matter what the auxiliary business may be, or how sorely it may press upon the over-burdened body and mind, it gradually becomes a necessity, reckoned upon as an essential part of the income, and impossible to be done without. That such work is an evil of the first magnitude cannot be gainsaid by any thinking man. Unless of course it be, as sometimes happens, in the nature of a recreation, but even then what home life can the man have who is absent at work from breakfast time until nearly mid-night? And what justice can he do his legitimate employer, who after all has the best right to his chief energies.

It may be said that if men were only paid a sufficient wage for the work they do during the day they would not seek evening employment, but such a statement would be very difficult to prove, since what is sufficient for one is not for another. And some men have a mania for work, begrudge themselves necessary sleep and food time, not because they *need* the money, but because they *want* it. The best that can be said for the practice is that it is far better than spending every evening in the vicious atmosphere of a saloon bar or public billiard-room, as so many workers do under the plea of recreation. But both are bad for the man practising them, making him prematurely old, and robbing him of all real enjoyment of life.

And yet how great is the excuse for the poorly paid clerk, who, having married and seeing his children coming all too quickly, is at his wit's end to know how to meet his ever growing expenses upon a non - expanding salary. I know for a fact that an enormous majority of the married clerks and salesmen of London live the life of slaves to those whom they love, toiling ever with one end in view, the comfortable maintenance of their dear ones. In literature, save the mark, they are held up to scorn and ridicule, the clerk and the " counter jumper " being taken as fair game for every smart pen, and even giants of the quill like Mr H. G. Wells do not scruple to draw such a hideous caricature of a splendid solid class as Kipps. A monstrous exception if ever there was one to the great rule that these hardly entreated workers are fit to hold their own in any society, and as far as their work is concerned need not fear comparison with any.

To resume, as far as I am personally concerned, I found that even the trifling amount that I was able to add to my income by my infrequent sales of fancy goods for monthly payments, became absolutely necessary to me, and I craved too for some means of adding thereunto. I answered many advertisements, but they were all of the canvassing or touting order, and I felt that I could much easier starve than do that. Why, I always found it a dreadful task to go on board a ship, and ask if they wanted any hands, to offer myself for hire ! and that compared to the door to door canvassing is ridiculously easy. However, I was fortunate enough to get a job now and then to write up some firm's advertisement books, and so utilise the holidays I was allowed, but could not enjoy. This, and addressing envelopes at 3s. 6d. per thousand (I believe it is now done for 1s. 6d.), brought in a little valuable money, and improved my handwriting too. And still I craved for more. For one thing my seafaring habit of early rising clung to me so, that I simply could not remain in bed even on the dark mornings of winter after six o'clock, while in summer I was often out and about at three, enjoying the freshness of the young day, but lamenting that I could not put this leisure time to some presently profitable use. It was the same in the evening. Beyond the open-air meetings on Sunday and Thursday, I had no recreations, no places of amusement. I could not read *all* the time, and although I walked fully ten miles a day to and from my work I had abundant energy still available.

Now among my many deficiencies I was always painfully conscious of a lack of mechanical genius, or even aptitude. As before noted, I could not drive a nail without bending it, or turn a screw without burring the head. Yet one day it chanced that I stood in the shop of an acquaintance of mine watching him make picture - frames, and the thought occurred to me that I could learn to do likewise, and thus perhaps utilise my spare time, and earn a little money into the bargain. Thenceforward I was a frequent visitor to him, and my questions were many, but, such was my shyness that I never asked for a practical lesson.

While in this absorbent frame of mind a canvasser called at our office with some rather good steel engravings for sale. They were in monthly parts of three in paper portfolios with descriptive letterpress, and were entitled the " Imperial Gallery of British Art." Price five shillings per part, the series to be completed in sixteen parts. As I looked at the beautiful pictures, for, in spite of worn plates and retouching, many of them *were* beautiful, a scheme sprang to being in my brain. Why should I not subscribe for two sets of engravings, frame them myself, and sell them on my monthly payment system? In about five minutes I had decided that I would venture, and had signed a document burdening me with the payment of ten shillings monthly for sixteen months.

After this, I suppose it is useless for me to say that I have or had no speculative instinct, since I thus determined upon so slight a prospect to mortgage such a considerable sum out of my income. But I think it must have been some long dormant *flair* for business which thus suddenly materialised. However that may be, I was for the time being possessed by my scheme, and frequented the shop where my friend was always making frames more assiduously than ever. I plied him with questions innumerable, all of which he answered very readily, seeing in me a good prospective customer for material in order to carry out my hobby, as he supposed it to be, and never even dreaming that I might be a possible business competitor.

I afterwards found that amateur picture frame-makers when properly encouraged make exceedingly good clients to the professional, whose aim it should be to encourage them by all the means in his power to make their own frames. Because it is almost certain that the amateur will spoil far more material than he uses, and that his friends to whom he shows his work with pride will make mental notes of his great inferiority to the work of the professional, and determine never to have any home-made frames themselves. This attitude of the professional towards the amateur is an exceedingly profitable one, and pervades a

F

great many trades, where it is recognised that the man with a hobby is a sort of bubbling well from whence the judicious fosterer of his client's most amiable weakness may draw an ever - increasing profit.

Of course I made mistakes at starting, which cost me far more than I could afford, mistakes which I should not have made had I possessed any mechanical genius whatever.   But I had what was better, an imperative necessity to succeed.   You remember the story of the cow climbing the tree ?   It was exactly my case. There was no question of my learning to frame pictures, I had to.   But for that I know should have flung down my tools and upset my glue-pot early in the game, vowing solemnly that to learn such a business was impossible at my time of life and as a side issue.   But I did not, because I dared not, and after spending about six times their value in moulding, and forty times as much in hard, almost despairing work, I at last emerged from the struggle with two framed pictures.

Looking back now I am amazed at even that moderate measure of success.   For we only had three rooms, and I had two children.  Consequently my only workshop was the apartment which served us as kitchen, dining-room, and living room.   The Pembroke table, all rickety as those abominations always are, was my bench, and not infrequently capsized with all my litter of work upon it.   Of the usual appliances for the work I had scarcely any. For instance I have often, to their great delight, used my two children for a press—that is to sit on the board in order to keep newly pasted down engravings or photographs from cockling up. And if when putting the back into a frame I accidentally touched the glass with the point of a brad, hearing at once the ominous click which told me I had lost sixpence, the price of the square of cheap glass, my children's hilarity was hushed in a moment as they saw the almost despairing look in my eyes, and the haggard expression on my face.

But I am getting on too fast. So much depends upon the point of view, so relative are our joys or sorrows to our circumstances that I doubt whether Columbus upon first beholding that will-o'-the-wisp-like light upon San Salvador was more elate than I when I first beheld the two finished frames which were the work of mine own hands. True I had bought the moulding, and the gold or gilt slip. True I had bought the ready cut mount from another tradesman, and the squares of glass had been cut to my measurements by another, but mine was the hand that had, after much bungling and patching and besmearing of thick glue, achieved those frames. I felt that I could not weary of looking at them. Mine was the joy of creation, however lawlessly assumed. Upon rising at five the next morning, before dressing I paid a visit to them for another admiring survey, and a wondering retrospect as to whether it was really I who had succeeded in producing two such works of art. Of course I had nothing to compare them with, but that was the merest detail, it troubled me not at all.

I was all impatience to get to the office with them, nor, although I am the least optimistic person alive, could I feel any great amount of trepidation as to whether they would be favourably received or not. It was a long and weary walk across the park from Kilburn to Westminster, and my hands were blue with the cramping cold through carrying my precious pictures, but I cared nothing for that. I was for the time being satisfied with myself. And yet as I drew near the office where my amateur work would be submitted to the shrewd if not unkindly judgment of my fellows, and I should learn once for all whether in the city man's phrase there " was money in it," I had hard work to keep my spirits up. Fortunately I did not know what the odds were against me, a blissful ignorance which has saved many a struggler from collapse of dread before the fight has begun.

It is just possible that my work of totalling and meaning massive columns of figures, mechanical and monotonous as it had become, suffered that morning from utter lack of any ability on my part to think of what I was doing. But at last the luncheon interval of three quarters of an hour came, and having bolted my usual dinner of bread and cheese, I began my tour of the various rooms with my work. I sold my pictures to the first man I showed them to at a good profit on the usual terms of five shillings a month, but he very kindly allowed me to tote them all round the office, by which means I secured orders for six more. Better than that I heard words of praise to which I had almost always been a stranger, praise of my work, at which I was far too gratified to inquire whether those who uttered it were competent critics, or were trying to get my wares a little cheaper, or on a little easier terms. It was a day to be marked with a white stone, and I find it impossible now to recall any definite idea of the multitudinous schemes of infinite pettiness which that day's success hatched in my brain. I can only say that in their prospective wealth of a few shillings extra a week, they were just as important, I was just as earnest in considering them, as any millionaire manipulator of stocks and shares, even though he looks for more tens of thousands from other people's labour than I looked for units from my own.

Behold me then launched as a (vide my cards printed soon after) " Carver, gilder, and picture-frame maker. Clients visited at their own residences. Advice upon all art subjects gratis; estimates free!" Nevertheless I found it anything but plain sailing. At almost every turn I came up against some problem that would have given me no trouble had I served a year

in a bona fide frame-maker's shop. Mostly I got
over or round the difficulty somehow by myself, for
I grew more and more diffident of asking for instruction at the shop where I bought my moulding and
et ceteras. But I was steadily improving in my work,
steadily learning more and more of the details of the
business, and gradually acquiring more tools suitable
for the work. It is often scornfully said to the amateur,
who is lamenting his inability to do better because
of the want of proper tools, that a " bad workman
always blames his tools." That may be true, but it
is certainly not truer than that no regular workman
would attempt to commence a job with the tools
that the average amateur possesses. Bad or good
as the result may be, that there is any result at all
from amateur work proves the possession of what
all are agreed that the workman is always the better
for, a love of the work for its own sake, and not
at all from any hope of reward for his achievement
outside of the satisfaction of his own innate desire
for perfection.

I was now much happier. I cannot conscientiously
say that I loved the new work for its own sake, but
I had never enjoyed the possession of a hobby except
reading and open-air preaching, and I was as I have
said far too poor to indulge my tastes even in these
pursuits to the full. But I was certainly interested
in pictures and their frames. I was both surprised and
delighted to find that I actually had some mechanical

skill after all, and I never felt quite satisfied that my work was as well done as possible. By which of course I mean that I was always striving to do it better; not only, I can safely declare, because of pleasing a customer, but for the great delight of admiring the work of my own hands before I delivered it over to its owner.

Moreover, I found to my deep gratification, that my circle of acquaintances or I may say even, friends, which had been exceedingly small, was now being constantly enlarged. Nearly every new customer I obtained became interested in the man beyond his work, and this intercourse though it undoubtedly took up a great deal of time was very pleasant. Before long I was adding a few shillings regularly every week to my income, every one of which represented a great deal of work and scheming and persuasion; shillings that were well and faithfully earned, if ever shillings were. I did most of my work in the morning before going to the office, for after office hours I was handicapped by the fact that I had to go to the city to buy my mouldings and mounts, or to make long journeys with the finished product.

This gathering together of the material that I used was one of the chief drawbacks to my progress. I could not of course lay in a stock; first, because I had no capital; secondly, because I had no room to store it; and thirdly, because, owing to the enormous variety of patterns, I could never tell what I should want a stock of. Of course I early learned to guide my client's taste in the direction of the easily obtainable (and profitable to me) patterns for obvious reasons, but if a customer had seen a certain pattern and required it, I never tried to persuade him out of it, but did my very best to satisfy him. Here I found another enormous difficulty. I did not know what to charge! There was no one of whom I dared ask the question, for it will be quite easily understood that in all trades there must be intense jealousy and dislike of an outsider coming in by a side entrance and cutting into the business. I got some help from the price-lists of the great stores, finding that I could make a very respectable profit, as I considered it, by charging about twenty-five per cent. less than they did. But that only helped me a little way, because I was continually confronted by the cheap frames made by the gross and sold by the drapers and fancy goods people at a few pence and some farthings each, less in fact than I could buy the materials for in the making of one frame.

So I groped blindly along, sometimes making a fair profit on my labour, sometimes after two or three days' hard work emerging with about what I started with because of unforeseen difficulties. I may have undersold the legitimate operators in the same line, but if so it was entirely due to ignorance on my part—I would never willingly spoil any man's market, unless of course as in some monopolies prices needed reduction in the interests of truth and honesty.

The writing of the last three words of the preceding sentence has suddenly brought before me the necessity of a word or two of explanation. I have not the slightest intention in these chapters to be dictative. Still less do I wish to write a clumsy tract. And yet I find upon looking back upon the last few pages that I am in great danger of being accused of a snug and disgustingly hypocritical trumpeting forth of my virtues. From such a peril I desire to guard myself if possible. And I feel that I can only do so by stating definitely that although of course I claimed to be a Christian man, my actions with regard to my work did not seem to me to spring from any desire to follow a certain code of moral laws, but to do to others as I wished they would do to me. At my proper work at the office I know I was often indolent and careless, and pre-occupied with my own affairs when I ought to have given my best abilities to the duties for which I was paid, the reason (not the excuse) being, that I never could take the slightest interest in it. But in my private business outside the office I did always try to give the best possible value for the money I received, and I had an absolute horror of overcharging anybody.

Moreover, on certain occasions when I had to pay others to do what I could not do myself, and based my proposal for payment on the profit I expected to make, I have several times, on finding that my profits were larger than I had expected, voluntarily increased the payment to my helper. Not, I affirm, because of any deep-seated desire to be just as well as kind, but, because it was the easiest way to quiet some inner impulse driving me in the direction of justice. This is not a matter of virtue, it is a matter of temperament. There is to me something diabolical, infernal, in the idea of " doing " anybody, of getting the better of them in a business deal, of binding men down to serve you for a pittance upon which they can hardly live, and making yourself a fortune by their labour. And I believe that a faithful servant who puts love for you as the employer into his or her work is valuable beyond all payment, but that fact should never hinder the recipient of such service from paying as liberally as he can, not caring a hang for the laws of political economy.

Dear me, how far this kind of thing does lead one to be sure. But I have the most vivid recollection of those reflections in that strenuous time, and they gave point and edge to my remarks made on Sunday morning at Kensal Green Cemetery Gates, to the immense audiences of men waiting there for William the Fourth to open. I preached the doctrine of Christian Socialism as I saw it, as different from the naked and unabashed Socialism of the Keir Hardie type, as light is from darkness, a social law of love and duty towards my neighbour, whether he be rich or poor. And this was a great and splendid compensation, even when as often happened, I, having laid out my last few shillings on Friday for materials wherewith to make frames in the hope of getting paid for them on Saturday, found that I was left with only a few pence to procure that sacrament of the Londoner, the Sunday's dinner.

However hard those times now seem to look back upon, I can very plainly see how much of pleasure and good training there was in them, compensations of which I then thought little. But I cannot help seeing also how helpful a few business-like habits would have been. I cannot say that I had a rooted objection to keeping accounts, I only know that I never did keep them except in my head. And consequently I grew to trust my memory for everything, which in business, however small, is I now know fatal. Yet I know, too, that had I been managing anybody else's business, I should have been a scrupulous book-keeper. Blamable in the last degree this constitutional aversion of mine from putting down what I had spent and how much I had earned from that spending. Also, for another confession, though I was in theory anything but an optimist, in practice I acted optimism. I never could feel sure of my monthly government pay, until I had actually cashed the cheque, yet in the face of demands which it seemed miraculous that I should ever be able to satisfy I was cheery, even confident, that, as Dickens so scornfully puts it, " things would come round."

Now I must close this chapter, already overlong,

but before I do so I must just say that at this time
I drank nothing but water or tea, did not smoke, never
paid a penny for recreation, and wore my clothes till
I dared wear them no longer.   And yet I was, with a
steady salary of £2 2s. a week, abjectly poor !

# CHAPTER VII

## I TAKE A SHOP

LAST chapter closed with a bitter confession of incompetence on my part that I would not make if I could help it, but alas it is too true. Account for it I cannot, except by saying that I began by getting into debt, as I have before said, and never afterwards until the end of that régime came was I able to emerge from the condition of poverty I have attempted to describe, not though my struggles were incessant and certainly severe. It tinged my whole life and robbed me of my rightful proportion of joy, this want of ability to manage my own affairs upon a very small and strictly stationary income. If this condition of things may be taken for granted, whether with blame or pity, it will simplify matters a good deal and save me humiliating allusions to it every now and then.

So time fled along in rapid fashion, for now I never had a moment to spare. And still further to curtail the time at my disposal, I, finding the burden of the rent in the west of London too grievous to be borne, to say nothing of the cruel anxiety of letting lodgings unfurnished, decided to migrate to the far east of

London, between Upton Park and East Ham. There I had heard that a neat five-roomed house with a long garden could be hired for seven and six a week inclusive of all rates and taxes. (I believe the same house would fetch nearly if not quite double now.) That was a rental I felt able to pay, and even if the great distance from my employment did mean extra expense, it was well worth a struggle to have a home to ourselves freed from the incubi of lodgers or sub landlord.

So with great hopes of making the last move for a long time, I commenced the big business. It must be confessed that the auspices were not very bright, my wife being too ill to stand upon her feet, my eldest child a toddler of five, and my next one quite a baby. But in those days such details hardly fretted me, I was so used to them. And consequently it was with a stout heart that, having succeeded in hiring a big van and horse and man, at one and sixpence an hour, I commenced the long day's labour at seven in the morning. I carried my wife and little ones into a good Samaritan next door, who looked after them, while my helper and I dismantled the home and carefully stowed it in the van. For once I had found a man who was willing to work as hard as I could, and who did not seize every opportunity to suggest rest and refreshment. So we got on very well indeed.

By nine o'clock all was ready, my wife was comfortably secured upon a sofa lashed to the tailboard of the van, the baby was accommodated with an impromptu cot on the keyboard of the piano, and the five-year-old also had a place for her little chair. So we started off for our new home facing the twelve miles between us and that distant suburb without misgivings, though it was certainly anything but a picnic for the horse. I do not recall how many times we halted, only I know that but few of them involved the spending of money, that being as usual a very limited quantity with me. But at five o'clock the weary trudge was over, and, with fresh energy we tackled the task of getting the chattels indoors. With such good will did we both work that by six all was over, and the hard-working carman, apparently satisfied with my moderate tip of a shilling, and sixteen and six for the hire of the vehicle, departed and left me to the tackling of my biggest task of the day.

I felt as if I would much rather lie down and rest, but it is astonishing what you can do when you must, and finding fresh energy somewhere I soon had the helpless wife and children fairly comfortable, with a bit of fire in a bedroom. While thus engaged I was drawn to the window by a tremendous crash of thunder and flash of lightning, and there, outside one of the opposite houses, was ranged on the pavement nearly the whole of a family's furniture exposed to the full fury of a torrent of rain. Indeed it was pitiful, and my discontent at the heavy task before me was changed into great gratitude when I realised what I had escaped from by only a few minutes.

I went back to my work with a good heart, and before midnight, when dead beat, I crawled into bed and fell at once into a sleep so sound that even the heavenly artillery failed to disturb me, I had reduced my new abode to something like order. I was up again at 5.30, having ever been able, no matter how weary, to rise at any time necessary, and after another hour's work at straightening things out, sallied forth to find someone who would come and help my helpless ones during my absence. This I fortunately succeeded in doing in time, and at 7.30 I was on my way to the office looking forward to a good rest for my muscles all day, even if my brain would certainly be superlatively active.

Now I am quite well aware that in chronicling the above I am laying myself open to the charge of being jejune, trivial, etc., and I know too, that to many men of my own class such details as I have given above will be so familiar that they will wonder why ever I should have written about them. But somehow I have felt that, as in the subjects of my other books, a little plain and simple truth amidst the flood of invention by writers who have merely looked on, might not be out of place, might indeed be of use. For I hold that it is impossible, even for those who are most interested but do not live the life, however keen they may be, to portray faithfully all the day and night doings of the people they write about. They may and do try hard and honestly to fulfil their self-imposed task, but as long as they can retire to their comfortably furnished homes and nicely served meals whenever they like, they will never be able to describe truly, however much they wish to do so.

For a little while the novelty of setting my house in order and the delight of having a garden for the first time in my life prevented me from dwelling upon the obvious disadvantages of the change of abode I had made. But when I came to realise that in order to live at a low rent·and have a little house to myself I had to put in nearly four hours a day travelling, I began to wonder whether I had not been foolish after all. This was long before the days of the extension of the District Railway to East Ham, and I could only keep my travelling expenses within possible limits by taking a workman's ticket, not available after 7 A.M., to Fenchurch Street, and walking thence to Victoria. This long journey, during which I was perforce idle, played havoc with my business of picture-framing, yet still I managed to keep my hand in, and indeed improved a little in that I had a small workshop to myself now, and no longer made frames on the kitchen table.

And I should be ungrateful indeed if I did not remember most affectionately the delights of Wanstead Park and Epping Forest. Many and many a pilgrimage I made in the summer with the children packed

G

in a big perambulator and a bag containing all the materials for a homely picnic slung on the handles to those sylvan glades, and here, at no other expense save the muscular effort, enjoyed a delightful holiday, the best perhaps I have ever known, because purely unconventional and costless. I had the satisfaction of feeling too that, in spite of the rapidity with which streets of small houses like the one I was living in were springing up all around me, the grand forest would never be built on any more, would always be available for such poor workers as myself.

Nevertheless I confess I did mightily begrudge the great waste of time involved in my much travelling. In the summer it was not so bad, but in winter I and many more in like case, who for motives of economy got to our respective places of employment long before we could get in, suffered much from lack of shelter from cold and wet. Just one of the many unconsidered evils of living in a vast and over-crowded city. My extra work of picture framing suffered also, not merely because customers in my new neighbourhood were exceedingly scarce, everybody being so poor, but because of the long, long distance I had to fetch materials, especially glass, which in the crowded trains at night was a most ticklish and brittle load. I cannot now realise definitely the sudden rushes I used to make through the heart of the city at the busiest hour of the evening, my struggle with the clambering crowds up the steep stairs in Fenchurch

Street Station, and the journey homewards in the close-packed, reeking compartment, dreading every moment lest a lurch of the train should damage my precious burden. It is all like some hideous nightmare, those wet and foggy nights when my lungs seemed fit to burst with coughing, and all my senses warned me to go slow, while my needs spurred me, and many times I had to stop and remember how many were in far more evil case than myself, or I should have indeed fallen by the wayside.

Yet this life too I endured for three years, at the end of which time I was fully convinced that living so far away from my daily work was for me at anyrate a profound mistake. Also I had another child and was in consequence driven harder than ever, was more desirous than ever to have some steady auxiliary to my exiguous income, some means of getting clear of that furniture incubus which kept my nose to the grindstone. Besides all these things I had often in winter, despite my early leaving home, to spend several hours on the way to the city by reasons of floods, to which our neighbourhood then seemed particularly liable, and had been curtly warned by the Powers above me that I would do well to move nearer to my work if I wished to retain it. Which warnings gave me a cold chill at the heart, for although I was in age not much past thirty, I was already beginning to feel old from the strain of living, and I knew how scanty were the chances of getting another such berth as mine should I lose the one I had now got.

But I doubt whether even these powerful incentives to a change would have been sufficient to make me move, but for an event which changed the whole course of my life. For one thing, where was I to go and enjoy better conditions than those under which I now lived? Even apartments were now not to be thought of, for I had three children, and except in such neighbourhoods as I dared not descend to, no one would let apartments to people with a family. This again is one of the factors governing the lives of the workers which those comfortable souls who wail about the declining birth-rate do not think of. God knows it is hard enough for any poor worker in England to maintain a growing family in decency, without being treated worse than a beggar or a criminal in seeking to find lodgment for them which he is ready to pay for. Thousands of men have been driven to pauperism or practical socialism by the accursed system of oppression — no children wanted.

So that every enquiry I made about lodgings nearer my work threw me back to the grim fact that in some respects, I was better off now than any change could make me. And then came the event, the impulse from without, which drove me against my own better judgment into the thorny and difficult ways of the

I TAKE A SHOP

small shopkeeper. My wife received a small legacy, one that had been left contingent upon the death of a woman who enjoyed the income of the bequest for life. She died, and the capital was divided among a very large number of expectant folk, none of whom received, according to their ideas, much more than a tithe of what was really due to them. My wife's share was well under £200, but even that was a fortune to our entirely restricted vision. Of course the first and most important question to be decided was how to dispose of this money to the best advantage so that we might feel the benefit of it ? But underlying this there was a feeling upon my part that as it was not mine in any sense my wife should have the disposal of it, so long as she did not insist upon, as I once heard a County Court Registrar pithily remark, frittering it away upon paying my outstanding liabilities. No, I do not exactly mean debts, but in clearing up those burdens which demanded regular instalments of so much a month.

I am glad to say, however, that nothing was farther from her ideas than that, for as she put it, the furniture was all worn out long before it was paid for, being such utter rubbish, and therefore the longer its vendors could legitimately be kept waiting for their ill-gotten gains the better. Alas, to be wise after the event is futile, yet I am now sadly inclined to think that had such a proposal been made by her and accepted by me it would have been better for all of us. At anyrate this book would not have been written, nor, I feel certain, any other of the small library that I have written during the last ten years.

Her suggestion, no, it was more than that, it was a demand, was that this money should be laid out in taking a shop. A double-fronted shop whereof one side should be devoted to art pictorial in the shape of its accessories, engravings, frames, artistic materials, etc., and the other to what is rather pompously called art needlework, and fancy goods, the latter being an enormously elastic term.

To say that I was alarmed would be putting matters much too mildly. I was appalled. I dreaded beyond expression increasing my already heavy liabilities. I doubted with a scepticism of the blackest my ability to run a shop for myself, however well I might be able to do it for another—in fact, I saw nothing in the proposal but disaster. But my wife, confident in her powers as a shopkeeper (having had no experience) and fired with a laudable desire to help in the collection of the family income, insisted, even at the length of declaring that if I would not take a shop she would without my help. And that I saw would be avoiding an imaginary Scylla for the terrors of a real Charybdis. So I yielded, ungracefully, but completely, and thenceforward until the time which shall complete this narrative never did I know a care-free hour.

The first thing was to find the shop, and if I were

able in Mr Pett Ridge's delightful manner to detail our experiences in those pilgrimages I doubt not that the recital would make several readable columns. The lies we were told would fill several volumes. The fortunes we were sure to make were so vast that they were unspendable. Every miserable, little, obviously hopeless shop was lauded so that I began to fear a complete obsession, and at last I declared that I would not take any advertised business at all, I would build up a business of our own. Yes, I used those memorable words, and, to my shame be it said, without even the excuse that I believed them myself. Miserable man that I was, I felt certain that this enterprise of ours was foredoomed. I knew, none better, that there was nothing of the Napoleon about me, that I was far too prone to take no for an answer for anything of that kind to be possible.

Presently I began to feel that this quest of a shop was destined to bring me prematurely to my grave. East, west, north, and south I sought, and now I felt no nearer than at the outset to the object of my search. At last I found what apparently was exactly the thing, a double-fronted shop with a sufficient number of living rooms above, in a business thoroughfare within easy reach of town, and at the fairly reasonable rent of £40 a year. I knew no one who could tell me anything about the character of the neighbourhood, so I had to form my own conclusions as to the prospects of business there. And in any case I was so weary of searching for the apparently unattainable that I was willing to be deceived had anybody tried to persuade me. But that I think was the determining factor. Nobody did try to influence me. The man who owned the shop and carried on the business of a grocer next door did not seem at all anxious to have me for a tenant, in fact he was most reticent and retiring when approached, which may have been genius on his part, although I never saw cause to suspect him of anything of the kind.

At anyrate I persuaded myself that I should never find any better shop than this for my purpose and I closed the bargain by paying handsel, and fixing the date for coming in. Then I had to turn my attention to the fitting up of this shop, for it was absolutely bare, just three match-boarded walls which by the way were covered with some messy alleged varnish which never dried, and the double front as aforesaid. I procured several price-lists from firms whose speciality was the fitting up of shops, and after a prolonged study of them came to the conclusion that to fit up this shop in even the most economical way, according to their specifications, would absorb our entire capital and necessitate our procuring stock entirely on credit. Which was absurd ; for we had no credit, at least in my innocence of business I knew of none. Later, I learned to my sorrow that the obtaining of credit was easy in almost an exactly inverse ratio to the difficulty of meeting the bills when they came in.

In this difficulty of fitting the shop, however, as in so many others that I have encountered, I had not the privilege of retreat. I had burned my bridges and had perforce to advance in what at first appeared to be a hopeless task. But I am getting on too fast, for of course, before I could begin shop-fitting it was necessary that I should move in, this operation being in itself, with my limited resources, a sufficiently formidable one. But here again, I met with a powerful co-adjutor in the man that used to serve us with vegetables and coals at Upton Park, a burly costermonger who had risen to the dignity of a little shop and a horse and van from the humble beginnings of a hand-barrow. It was his proud boast that he would rather at any time go hungry himself than refuse a poor customer half a hundred of coals or a few pounds of potatoes because she had no money. He and I often had a yarn and had become great friends, so that when I enlisted his aid in moving the long distance from Upton Park to Lordship Lane, East Dulwich, I felt that relief which only comes from implicit reliance upon someone whom you feel is stronger than yourself. I know all about self-help and have been compelled to practice it all my life, but the joy of having a friend, how great and how pleasant it is !

With his powerful aid the moving out was got over with comparative ease, but even so, it was dark before we arrived at our destination, the children being cold, tired, and hungry. And then a difficulty occurred which almost daunted me. I had the key of the shop, but my landlord had bolted up inside so that I could not get in. And when I went to him he offered me my handsel money back, mumbling something about " matters not being satisfactory." What he meant I do not even now know but that was what he said, and there was I in the street with all my belongings, ten miles from the home I had left at 8 A.M. and with three small children. My friend and ally here arose to the occasion. He literally bullied the landlord into letting us in, a thing I could never have done, and presently I found relief from my anxiety in the feverish activity of getting our chattels indoors. I never heard, and so I can never tell, why my landlord desired to evade his bargain regardless of my sufferings, nor, although I even now feel curious, shall I ever know.

Oh, that good fellow, how he did work as if he had just begun his day instead of having been at it since about 4 A.M. He helped me set up the beds, straighten up a living room, lit a fire, fetched some supper from a local pork butcher's, and at last with an earnest enquiry as to whether he couldn't do anything more for me, supposed he'd better be getting towards home as he had to be up at three the next morning. Falteringly I assured him that he had done far more than I could ever have expected and what was I in his debt ? he said brusquely, " Oh, I ain't got no time to bother abart that nar. You get strite an' I'll pop over an' see yer in a few dyes. Good night missus, good night guvnor," and he was gone. It was two months before I saw him again, and then only because I sought him out in my first leisure. And he would not take a penny more than ten shillings. I paid him that, but I have never discharged, because I cannot, the heavy debt of gratitude he laid upon me, more especially for the knowledge of how good and kind one poor man can be to another. I have had many such experiences, but each one has been peculiarly fragrant, especially sweet in itself, a standing rebuke to me for once holding a doctrine of the innate depravity of mankind.

As soon as he had gone I realised that I was so tired that I could hardly stand, and so I made haste to put things in readiness for the morning and get to bed. But once there my life-long habit asserted itself, and I had to find a book for a little read before sleep. And to my great content I found Mark Twain's " Innocents at Home," and read for perhaps the hundredth time the touching story of Scotty Briggs and the callow minister. In it I forgot my troubles, my weariness of body and mind and apprehensions for the future, and with a happy sigh I laid the book down, blew out the candle, and went to sleep. Years after, dining with Mark Twain at the Devonshire Club, I told him of the incident and saw his deep tender eyes fill with tears. He silently put out his hand and said " shake." Now can there be any higher reward for a writer than this, that he has been able by his books to make his fellow-creatures forget for a while the burden that has been crushing them, and has lifted them into new hope and energy for the coming unknown day ?  I think not.

# CHAPTER VIII

## GETTING BROKEN IN

THIS, the most momentous move of my life, as I think, was made on a Monday in the autumn of about 1890. The year doesn't matter anyhow. I know that it was about sixteen or seventeen years ago, or when I was thirty-three or thirty-four years of age. That Monday I had taken leave from the Office, the day being deducted from my allowed twenty-eight days of summer vacation, as was customary with us. By favour of the authorities we were even allowed to take half days of leave, which prevented us from doing what we believed our happier brethren in the *pukka* Civil Service could always do, ask to step out after lunch and not come back that day. It also I suppose preserved as much of our self-respect as was possible, for we were thus able to say that we at anyrate did not rob our masters the public of any of our valuable time.

This reserve of time, however, was far too valuable commercially to me to be lightly drawn upon, and so, rising at five the next day, I did as much as possible towards getting straight before eight, when I started to walk to the Office, a little over four miles, but with the prospect of a long day's rest, as far as my body was concerned, in front of me. That week was one of the busiest in my whole life. My office work had to suffer, doubtless, for amid the dancing columns of figures or snaky automatic curves I could always discern the counters, shelves, showcases, etc., of this new daemon, the shop. Moreover, I had to interview wholesale people, dealers in art embroidery, crewels, etc., dealers in fancy goods, dealers in mouldings, etc., and open accounts upon the strength of that little capital, now fast dwindling away.

My education was rapid that week. I heard hundreds of new trade terms, of the existence of articles for sale of which I never before dreamed, of possibilities of profit making that were dazzling, and I remembered them all. But I kept no account of my growing liabilities, loading my memory with everything, and whenever an uneasy feeling persisted in making itself noticed that I was plunging far beyond my resources, I fell back upon the consoling hope that I should soon square everything when the shop was opened. And I had determined to open that shop on the following Saturday. I ordered a couple of thousand hand-bills advising the resident gentry of Slopers Island, as East Dulwich was then sarcastically called, that F. T. Bullen proposed opening the premises at 135 Lordship Lane, S.E., on Saturday next as a high class Emporium for the sale of fancy goods, and all the necessaries for the production of art needlework.

There was also a notice to the effect that Carving, Gilding, and Picture Frame Making, would be executed on the premises with promptness and dispatch, Artists Materials would be kept in stock, Oil Paintings restored, and their Frames Re-gilded, while expert opinion would be given free to would-be Picture Buyers, Amateur Framemakers would be supplied with materials at City Prices, and the Best Window Glass would be cut and sold. Builders supplied at Trade Prices. I need hardly say that I had advice in drawing up this precious circular or I should never have dared aspire to such sublime heights of mendacity— even now—though it is not easy—I blush to think on what a slender possibility of performance I based all those grandiloquent promises.

After all they did little harm. For I hired boys to distribute my bills in the best districts, paying them liberally upon their solemn promises to knock at each door, where there was no letter box, so as to make sure of my bills entering the houses. Next morning walking over Denmark Hill—it had rained somewhat heavily during the night—I saw my bills almost carpeting the sidewalk and roadway, and after my first bitterness of soul at the sad waste had passed off, I accepted the situation as a judgment on me from above for my shameless exaggerations. I never consoled myself by thinking of the specious and spacious lies of the Company promoter, the sufferers from which all contributed to his wealth, out of which he often gave liberally to religious institutions and felt a perfect glow of satisfaction thereat. But for all my experience I was both ignorant and simple, which may serve as a reason for my penitence, but no excuse.

The opening day arrived—I had been up nearly all the previous night putting the finishing touches to the appearance of the shop and the arrangement of the stock, and flattered myself that it looked pretty well. My wife, who had an innate genius for art needlework, was in charge of that department, and we had arranged that in the event of orders for picture framing coming in with an overwhelming rush, she was to promise, in case the customers would not accept her assurance that I would do the work as cheaply as possible from the patterns they might select, that I would wait upon them at their residences later on.

So I left that morning for the Office, standing for a moment on the opposite side of the Lane, to gaze with pardonable pride upon the bright shop with its blue and gold Fascia of

" ART NEEDLEWORK BULLEN AND PICTURE FRAMING."

It *did* look pretty, and although anything but an optimist I confess I did hope that its attractions would be irresistible to the passers-by ; he or she, especially she, would feel compelled to come in and buy something. Of course, being an eminently genteel concern I could not have, in the usual suburban fashion, a band of music performing in the first floor front with the windows open, nor two or three raucous voiced men exchanging witticisms with the passers-by upon their stupidity in missing an opportunity like this of parting with their brass with a thousand to one chance of getting the best value for it in the 'ole world, and if I could have there was no money to pay for it. But I confess that as I stood and looked at the pretty little show, I had a vision of past experiences in raging seas among savage men amid primitive conditions where life depended upon muscle and sinew and grit, and I felt indeed as if I had sold my birthright for a mess of pottage, or rather the promise of it, since it certainly was not yet delivered.

It was my long Saturday at the Office—for in these days we only had alternate Saturday afternoons off —and how I got through it I do not know. I expect I sorely vexed those above me by the frequency of my errors. But I pictured my wife with the shop full of eager buyers utterly unable to cope with the rush of trade. I built castle after castle in Spain, I was retiring from the office to take charge of an ever increasing business demanding all my energies, and building up a competency for my old age.

At last five o'clock came and I hurried homewards full of conflicting emotions. But never in my deepest

H

pessimism had I allowed myself to contemplate the reality as it confronted me upon arrival at the shop. At that time on Saturday afternoon there was not a single person in front of the shop, nor when I entered was there anyone inside ! I passed through into the parlour and enquired in a subdued manner what the day's fortune had been. I learned at once that not a single person had entered the premises that day with the idea of buying anything. There had been several beggars and people asking for change (they could hardly have come to a more hopeless place on such a quest since our total stock of currency was less than five shillings) but customers—none.

I was staggered, for I was unprepared. Nevertheless I put as good a face upon it as I could and solaced myself with some tea. But it was rather a mournful meal for the thought would continually obtrude itself " if this is the beginning what will the end be like " ? However, there was still plenty to do in the " getting straight " process, and being busy at that I had no time to brood over this inexplicable repugnance of the public to patronise me. Not that it was a busy thoroughfare—far from it. Lower down some trade was being done, but up where I was it looked like a new neighbourhood, I could not realise that it was a London suburb with a great population. I did not then know that for some mysterious reason Lordship Lane, except in one very small section of it, had always been shunned by shoppers, who went

` much farther afield to do their purchasing, down to Rye Lane, Peckham, or even as far as Brixton.

So that sad day closed with never a potential buyer, and that delicate perishable stock staring at me like the fruit of a crime, while the gas from the six burners flared away as if rejoicing in the expense it was causing me. So at eleven o'clock, I closed the emporium, and basket in hand sallied forth to buy our frugal Sunday's dinner, thinking somewhat bitterly that people must have food and clothing, but art needlework and picture frames, being unnecessary luxuries, they had evidently decided to do without.

I went to bed that night with a heavy heart, because now the fact that I was in debt without hope of repayment stared me in the face, nagged at me, would not let me shut it out, and for once my hitherto unfailing solace, reading, was of no avail. At last I summoned up my mental resources, and determined that since I had done all I could, it was worse than useless to worry about the unfortunate result. Doubtless I had done wrong, but with the most innocent and praiseworthy intentions, and so I would sleep—and I did.

The next day, Sunday, was a gloomy one for me, for I knew no one in the vicinity, and missed sorely my usual happy association with some body of open-air preachers, and I felt almost outcast from human sympathy, which, though it may be a confession of weakness, I always had a craving for. But I got through the day somehow, my children wondering what made their father so dull, such bad company, and was heartily glad when bedtime came, and I could again seek the beautiful solace of sleep.

When I awoke again on Monday morning at five o'clock, and commenced to busy myself about the house, it was with a feeling that was new to me then, but which never left me during all the time that shop, like some infernal incubus, clung to my neck. It was a sense of utter hopelessness of ever doing any good in this business, coupled with the absolute necessity of going on with it. I know I may be thought a poor minded craven for being daunted in this wise thus early, but I must plead that I had a prophetic instinct, besides my tangible experience, and the grim fact of all these bills presently falling due. But I can honestly say that this sense of hopelessness did not, as far as I am aware, ever prevent me from doing my best and working my hardest to make the best of what I felt to be a very bad job.

When I got to the office I realised that the shop must be dismissed from my mind altogether while at my desk if I was to retain my post. For I could take no half measures; I must either not think about it at all or think of nothing else. So I took hold of myself resolutely, and fixed my mind on my work, compelling an interest in it that I had never been able to feel before. And it did me good in two ways.

It relieved me of the hateful round of useless thought about the shop, and it salved my conscience, which was worrying me very much about the way in which I was certainly neglecting my most important duties. But I found it pretty hard to answer the inquiries of one or two friends to whom I had confided my plans for going into business. I had to be frank with them as to what had happened, and also to feign a hope, which I did not feel, that things would soon improve.

However, taking things on the whole I felt much better in spirit when I returned home on Monday evening. I felt, that, knowing the worst, I could hardly help expecting a little improvement, and as to the future—well, that was hardly my concern now. So that I was almost cheerful when I entered the shop door, and not too much startled when my wife rushed to meet me beaming, and crying, " I've sold something ! " I was sorely tempted to be sarcastic but forebore, and merely said quietly, " I *am* glad to hear that, what have you sold ? " " One of those pretty photo-frames out of my window, and here's the money," producing a shilling, and pointing to the two frames which remained of the same kind. Then I laughed long and loud, for the irony of the situation went clean through me. She stared at me in bewildered fashion, saying, " What on earth is the matter with you ? " She evidently thought I was mad.

I answered, " Nothing, *I'm* sane enough, but seeing that our first business transaction in the shop is to sell an article for a shilling which cost us eighteen-pence, I do not know what I might have been if I hadn't laughed." And I have to laugh now when I think of it. That was our first customer, and she had a bargain. Somehow I persisted in looking at the transaction in a humorous light, and so it didn't hurt us, and presently fate made us amends by bringing a friend in who was to me for all those grievous four years a veritable godsend. He was, like myself, a stranger in the neighbourhood, indeed he was a stranger to London, having come up to take charge of a branch library. He " happened in " as the Americans say, just to ask if I had some kind of nails or screws or something like that, for he was an ingenious chap, and always doing something or other to make the temporary library over which he presided more fit for its purpose without too much extra expense.

We got into conversation quite easily, and he was speedily in possession of my story. For, I was literally aching to tell it to someone, and I could not have found a more sympathetic listener. He was, I think, one of those people who are often cruelly described as " nobody's enemy " but his own, but who should be better described as everybody's friend but his own, for a more unselfish chap never lived, and that character is, whatever its other faults may be, possessed of the golden virtue of helpfulness in an eminent degree.

Well, before we had been talking an hour he was installed as the friend of the family, in which unenviable position, as far as he was concerned, he reigned without a rival all the time we had the business. It was a bright and cheery episode, and did me more good than a hundred customers would have done, so that I went to bed that night feeling quite contented, and happy. I had found a friend who would be a friend indeed.

The first proof I had of the value commercially of my new friend's help was that coming in contact with so many people at the library, he recommended me as a picture-framer in season and out. Anyhow he got me work, which, whether it paid or not, was what I ardently desired. For while I was *doing* something I was, as Kipling says, swallowed up in the clean joy of creation, and nothing else then mattered very much to me. So gradually customers began to flow in, very gradually it is true, but they *did* come, and although my gains were small I made many good friends who did their best to recommend me to others. I had a workshop on the first floor which was a chosen haunt of my intimates, who, their work being done, used to come and perch amidst the unpicturesque litter and watch me at work, preferring apparently to be there in thirsty discomfort to being in the local saloon bar. But how they did smoke! We had a varied compound of odours up there, boiling glue, sour paste and general dustiness, but the whole rank compound was leavened, and I think purified, by tobacco smoke, diligently emitted by my friends as they watched me at work.

The curious part of these gatherings was that I had nothing to offer these guests, no refreshment, either wet or dry.   I was far too poor for that.   Not that any of them ever seemed to expect anything but a precarious seat on the edge of a box, or even standing room.   They brought their own tobacco and talked and smoked while I worked, and when at last the job was finished and I had to say, " Now, you fellows must clear out, I've got to take this job home," they would go reluctantly—except occasionally that some of them would insist upon lending me a hand with my load to the door of the house that I was bound to.   Ah, it was a strenuous time and full of worries, but I know now that it had its own peculiar charm and value, also a certain zest which I shall never know again.

Noble sportsmen spend huge sums and risk life and limb hunting game, I was gambling with my health and strength for an elusive stake, and, generally speaking, the odds were against me.   And what made the venture of more intense interest was of course the helpless dependents.   These made it impossible for me to halt even if, as often happened, I lost heart. It must be a good thing to be compelled to go on, it often makes a hero out of quite an ordinary person, raising him to heights of effort of which he never dreamed himself capable. All the more honour therefore to those, who, without these incentives, press forward to their goal in defiance of every hindrance.

I now began to realise in full measure the minor trials of the shop-keeper. The mere buying and selling, the commercial side of the business had in it a good deal of pleasure, but there was little in the more sordid details of keeping the stock dusted, the shop clean, the windows bright. Oh, those windows! they had a fascination for the children of the neighbourhood, whose chief delight appeared to be to get a lump of horse-dung or mud or filth of any sort and smear on them immediately after I had spent an hour's hard work in getting them clean. And I did begrudge the time for doing this, yet I couldn't afford to pay for having it done, that would indeed have been taking the exiguous gilt off the all too scanty gingerbread. And there was yet another prime difficulty. I dared not let a customer go who wanted anything that I had not in stock at the time, but would promise to get it whatever it was. And so I had to make continual rushes to the city after office hours, the travelling expenses almost invariably eating up double the profits, rather than have a customer go elsewhere and say that he or she could not get what they wanted from me.

This is the main difficulty of a suburban shop like mine was, started with insufficient capital, for it is impossible to keep a stock on hand sufficient to meet the needs of all customers, so vastly varied are the details of nearly every business now. But in this matter the wholesale dealers are kindness and courtesy itself. They might very well neglect the small, hardly beset trader, or refuse to supply him unless he gave a substantial order, but in my experience they are just as courteous and ready to meet the wants of the smallest of their customers as they are of the huge retailers who spend scores of thousands of pounds per annum with them. I always think of this when I read diatribes in the press about the laxity of British trade methods abroad, and wonder how much truth there can be in them.

This, however, is trenching upon the ground of high commercial politics, very far removed indeed from my feeble shopkeeping, and so I must needs return humbly to the principal difficulty encountered on the left hand side of my shop, or let us say grandiloquently, " The Fancy and Art Needlework Department." When customers began to come in we soon found that they almost invariably wanted something we had not got in stock, often something which we had never heard of, and when we hinted that the demand was infrequent or unusual, lifted shoulders and half-closed eyes proclaimed most eloquently profound disbelief in our statements, or an equally profound belief in our unfitness for the particular business in which we were engaged. I was often tempted to believe that ladies upon whose hands time hung heavy did of malice aforethought study our poor windows, and finding that something in the art needlework line which they knew of was not there (alas *that* was not difficult), would enter boldly and ask for it. If by some happy but unusual chance we had it, and displayed it triumphantly, nothing was easier than to decry its quality or tint or something, and retiring say that they would think about it. Doubtless in this employment there was great sport to be found, seeing the number of women who practised it, but it needed the exercise of much patience and amiability to take it politely when once we had begun to realise that it was a game to these folks, and nothing more.

Still I make no doubt but that this trial did us good, in that no one can exercise patience and politeness without becoming more patient and polite. Only when the making of a sale was almost imperative by reason of present need for money there was often a sick feeling at the heart upon realising that the comfortably dressed, bejewelled woman upon whom we were attending so assiduously had not the remotest idea of making a purchase, but was only passing the time away in what was to her a pleasant fashion. Such behaviour, so common among women of leisure, is hard enough upon paid employers of a shop, but it is very much harder upon such people as depend upon the scanty earnings of the shop itself. Ah well, it was only another of the lessons I was learning that, as a sardonic shopkeeper friend of mine said one day, a small trader in London must be a transgressor, in that his way was certainly hard.

# CHAPTER IX

## IN HARNESS

NOW indeed I began to realise, in spite of what I so often read in the daily papers, something of the optimistic pushfulness of the commercial traveller. The shop had not been open very long when they began to call, and such was their power of persuasion, so eager were they to sell me something, however little, so as to get a foot in as it were, that I often felt grateful that I was away all day. I left concise orders that nothing was to be bought, but on the occasions when I happened to be at home I felt so soft and yielding in the hands of these persistent pushers of their employer's wares that I could not but pity my wife, charged as she was with the duty of saying no to men who refused to recognise such a word as belonging to any language.

They were so polite, so gentlemanly, so pathetic, and so well informed. They seemed able to talk upon any subject, although they all had a marvellous knack of twisting any topic round to the one they were interested in. The luxuriance and fruitfulness of their imaginations, too, always impressed me, and although I always deprecated them wasting their time over so impecunious a tradesman as I was I had a good deal of joy in their company, bright and cheerful as it always was. But I have also to confess that they were dangerous counsellors. Their pleading for small orders, just one line, their utter indifference to the payment, making it so fatally easy to get into debt, I look back upon now with horror. And yet I suppose it is of the essence of business, this hopeful airy outlook upon life. I now see that I might have stocked my shop with the choicest products, might have made it glow again and—but never mind—that comes later. I am not, never was, a strong-minded person; except in certain very restricted directions I am exceedingly prone to take the line of least resistance, but I do feel just a little puffed up with the knowledge that I was so often able to say no and stick to it in spite of all the blandishments of those delightful drummers.

I had been about a year in the shop when I realised that I could no longer expect to do any good whatever with the fancy department. The Islanders had obviously no aspirations in the direction of crewel work, applique or any other form of art embroidery. Or if they had they did not consider that my emporium was the place to satisfy them. So I began to face the possibility of writing off all the expenditure on that side as a loss, and the only question was, whose? For beyond all controversy I was now in debt—how much I would not know, dared not contemplate. But as my picture-framing was still a going concern, and subject to sudden spasmodic accessions of trade, I was always kept on the tenterhooks of expectation —I dare not say hope—that one big order might put things right. In this I was doubtless somewhat encouraged by a sympathetic fellow-clerk, who used to suggest to me the possibility of my getting orders for frames to be exhibited say in all the stations from King's Cross to Aberdeen, and just for fun we often used to speculate upon the profits to be obtained from such a contract. I knew perfectly well that I stood not the slightest chance of getting such a bit of fat as such a contract would be, but I felt that it cost nothing to build a castle or two upon its possibilities, and so I did.

Indeed I wanted some romance in my grey life now, for I was getting hemmed in on every side. The rates kept going up, the gas bills were crushing, sickness was perennial with us owing to the bad drainage of the house, and to make matters very much worse, the structural conditions of the place rendered it barely habitable. The landlord would do nothing, and I could do nothing, towards making the house fit to live in; and in consequence, as he lived next door, our relations, as they say in the newspapers, were strained. I blamed him then, but now I repent that I did so, for he was a poor man also, and he must have often felt that his rent was in the greatest danger. As indeed it was, although I gratefully remember that I *did* pay him all that he was entitled to, not indeed without some slight coercion, but still I did pay.

Fortunately for me I had made the acquaintance of some religious bodies in the neighbourhood, and I had now some employment for my Sundays. This was a prime necessity for me, for I had never been able to go to church in the ordinarily accepted sense of the term. I wanted to be up and doing. And as I had been used to this for years I felt the loss of it very much on coming to East Dulwich. And until I had made myself known and received invitations to speak in the open air meetings, I was quite unhappy. For no matter how much else I had to do, this particular business seemed to be indispensable to my wellbeing, to supply a need that nothing else would. I suppose that many of our present Members of Parliament owe their positions to the same compelling desire of holding forth to their fellows in the open air forum, of seeing the effect that their oratory has upon their hearers. Now I am not going to recapitulate the experiences I have set down in the " Apostle of the South East," but only to point out that this life of mine was as you might say triangular. First in point of importance, but not I fear in consideration, was the office, when I drew my regular recurring pay. Next the shop, which I never knew whether to class as an awful incubus or a pleasant recreation (it was both at times), and lastly the evangelistic work in the open air which claimed most of my Sundays. I might perhaps make up the square by bringing in my domestic life, but that would involve writing of details that are quite private, and so I leave that side to be assumed as a sort of leaven running through the whole lump.

From which foregoing outlines it may be taken for granted that my life was fairly full, that I had no need to kill time. Yet so true is it that the busiest people are always those who seem to have time at their disposal, that I managed to keep up my reading, not merely of books but newspapers, and followed all the events of the day with the keenest interest. But this was not, as it never has been, from an ardent desire to educate myself, and reach out ambitiously after something better than I was doing. If in all I have written hitherto there is one word that can be construed into a vain-glorious asking for praise on account of my energy, my perseverance, my earnest desire to get on and all the rest of the nauseous twaddle, I beg my readers to forgive me, and to believe that I had not, never had, never can have the slightest intention of posing in this manner.

My *Apologia* must be this: I worked hard because I was afraid of the consequences if I didn't, not at all because I was naturally industrious, energetic, or ingenious, for I know that I was none of these

I

things, or rather that I had none of these fine qualities. I read whenever I could, whatever I could, because I loved reading for its own sake, and I read good stuff because I had a natural distaste for rubbish. A good book could and can still make me forget all earthly ills, all my surroundings, in fact make me cry and laugh and wonder, while a bad book makes me absolutely ill if I persevere in reading it.

To return to another development of my business as a picture-framer consequent upon opening a shop. Delightful people came in and talked, first about pictures and their frames, then about art in all its branches (which by the way necessitated me reading up "Art"), and then by an easy transition to any subject in which they were interested at that particular time. Sometimes these breaks in the greyness of everyday life were welcome, and led to most useful acquaintanceships and friendships; but sometimes when I had an order to finish and deliver for urgent reasons, I talked with a wild pre-occupied look and itching hands, longing to tell my suave interlocutor to go to Jehannum or elsewhere, and let me get on with my work, yet not daring to do so for fear of offending a potential customer.

Yet very often when such a one had given an order for a one-and-ninepenny frame and had gone away, my over-wrought nerves refused to allow me to finish

what I had in hand.  Because, principally, of the glass.
Now your born glass-cutter has no nerves, cannot
have.  In the nice handling of a diamond across a
virgin sheet of fifteen-ounce glass, the slightest
imaginative tremor must have fatal results, that is as
regards the profit to be made from clean cutting.
But this important matter must be much more
particularly explained, for to me it has often meant
the difference between profit and loss, to say nothing
of the pains I endured by reason of my inability to
swear—for only language lurid, loud, and long, could
relieve my labouring bosom, I felt sure, on many of
these occasions.

Be it known to you then that the ordinary picture-
framer's glass comes from Belgium in cases containing
I forget how many sheets each about fifty inches long
and thirty-six inches wide, and weighing roughly
fifteen ounces to the square foot.  The price per case
varies continually, but it may be safely assumed that,
given a *skilful cutter*, a retail price of twopence halfpenny a square foot will yield a profit of about twenty
five per cent.  Only, much of this glass has so many
air bubbles in it, is so uneven in thickness, that it can
only be used for pictures on the assumption that the
customer will not mind a bubble giving a sinister
twist to some character's eye in the picture, or in
certain lights, a series of blotches upon the whole
scene.  It is really window glass, but when Christmas

number plates must be framed in competition for about eighteenpence each, no poor framer can afford to regard trifles like that. And then its uneven substance in such large sheets makes the manipulation of it a matter of extreme difficulty except to those in constant practice and with highly trained skill. Now very early in my occupation of a shop I learned that I must give up my old fiddling system of buying my glass ready cut in Westminister and carrying it home, for many reasons, not the least of these being that I got no profit out of it.

So I bought a diamond for twelve and sixpence, and happened to get a very good one. Then I ordered a case of glass, and unconsciously with it I received a stock of trouble out of all proportion to any profit I was ever likely to make. Nothing that ever I undertook gave me so many tremors, cost me so much sweat, as did this truly diabolical business of glass-cutting. The rough case in which the sheets came standing on its edge at the end of the shop was to me the abode of devils—I approached it trembling, drew out a great wavering sheet, and lifted it on to the sloping table covered with baize which I had made. If I got it there all right I heaved a great sigh of relief, and usually went about some other job for a little while to steady my nerves before tackling the more important business of cutting. That is if there was no one waiting for a square. If there was, although my mouth was dry and my heart was thumping furiously against my ribs I had perforce to assure a jaunty air and even, God help me, hum a tune while my teeth almost chattered. "Conscience doth make cowards of us all," but so does poverty and dread of loss which can be ill borne, and I will back poverty to be the greater maker of cowards. I know it will be thought that I am making a lot of this trivial matter, but I solemnly declare that during my seafaring career, in the presence very often of the most appalling dangers, I have never felt the sickness of heart that has come over me when one of the huge sheets of glass, has, despite all my care, fallen in a heap of tinkling fragments from my shaking hands.

I have many memories of painful endurance connected with glass, but one stands out prominently from all the rest. It was on a Friday, and I had rather a large order in hand which if I got in that night I might reasonably hope to get the money for on Saturday, and so be ready for that rapidly recurring bug-bear, Saturday night. I had three original sheets of glass left in the case, ample to fill the order I had in hand, even with a little more than my average allowance of accidents. I was singing blithely at my work when the tell-tale bell over the shop door announced a customer. With a sigh I laid down my tools, for in the midst of a job like that at nine o'clock at night I dreaded interruption, the more that I usually found it profitless, trivial, and annoying. I found a man in the shop twiddling a piece of string in his fingers, and my heart sank, for I knew that meant glass cutting, my customers for glass nearly always bringing their dimensions on pieces of string. He asked me quietly for a strip of glass " that size " throwing the string on the counter, *that* size being four feet long, by four and a half inches wide. For one moment I meditated telling him to go elsewhere, but an infernal spasm of pride came to me for my undoing, and assuming an air of nonchalance to hide my smouldering rage I drew out the first of my three sheets and laid it on the operating table. I laid the cutting laths on it and drew my diamond along its surface for about a foot when click! it cracked diagonally across. There was a cry of sympathy from my enemy, but without a word I removed the pieces and drew out another sheet. That literally fell to fragments as I was lifting it on the table.

Now my nerves were fretted to fiddle strings, but with the calmness of despair I laid hold on the third and last sheet taking absolutely no heed of some remarks which the man was making behind me. I got that on the table all right and cut the strip off, but as I was handing it to him it fell in three pieces. I went on to cut another strip and the remainder cracked in two lines making it almost useless for any purpose. Then almost blind and deaf with suppressed rage and misery I turned to my customer saying in a queer sounding voice, " I've got no more glass to break, you'll have to go somewhere else." And then he said something, *I* don't know what it was, but I suddenly lost control of myself and poured forth my sentiments.

I was wrong, unjust, and rude, for it was certainly no fault of his, and I have no excuse whatever, but oh it was hard to have to spoil six or seven shillings worth of glass, to have ruined my chance of completing the order I had in hand, and, as far as I could see, to have jeopardised the poor kids' Sunday dinner—which was the unkindest stroke of all. He had no sooner gone, with his measly sixpence still in his pocket, than I shut up the shop, put away my tools, turned out the gas, and went to bed with a book. But it was long ere I could make any sense out of the printed characters—they all danced amid a glittering halo of broken glass.

I had made several spasmodic efforts next day to overtake the difficulty which had fallen in my way, but unsuccessfully, and at 9 P.M. having done all I could towards the order, short of getting the glass for it, was standing disconsolately by my bench fingering in my trousers pocket a shilling and a few coppers—all I had, on a Saturday night, to " get the things in," as we say, for Sunday. Suddenly there came shrilling up the stairs a cheerful whistle —four notes of the ascending diatonic scale—the

signal of my inestimable chum Bob from the library
over the way. It was literally what the Hindus call
a *Hawa-dilli*, a heart lifter, whenever I heard it, but
never more so than now. I gave the response, and
he came bounding up—full of beans as usual. " Well,
old stick, how—" and then he stopped, my haggard
look I suppose daunted him. " Why, what's up then ? "
he queried. " Broke all your glass ? " I nodded
gloomily, and then because I was selfish, and full
of my own trouble, I burst out and told him all.

He listened in silence, but with a face full of sympathy, and when I had finished he said, thrusting
his hands down deep into his pockets, " That's too
bad; and I haven't got three bob myself. But
wait a bit—I believe I can touch Curwen for a quid
till pay day—I'll be back in a minute," and he was
gone. He seemed to be back almost immediately,
with a joyful face, shouting, " All right, old man, here's
half the plunder," holding out half a sovereign to me.
Did I take it ? Certainly I did; the possibility of
not doing so never occurred to me, for I knew even
then that I would do the same as Bob had done had
I the opportunity. Yes, I took the money, and in
a few minutes had laid in my supplies for Sunday
with an easy mind, but without extravagance.

This which is noted as if it might be an extraordinary occurrence, was nothing of the sort. Something similar happened many times, indeed it was

a fair sample of the friendship I enjoyed with this particular man—a true fellowship which I am glad to mention as a sample of the goodwill existing between chums, and as far removed from the cold-blooded so-called charity of the majority of those who have great possessions as can well be. If I dared I would like to add to it by giving some instances of similar kindnesses received from one or two others, not perhaps quite so intimate, but quite as kindly meant, and as spontaneously offered. Only, alas, I know that to be more explicit upon this head would be to offend those generous hearts most grievously. They belong to the small select class who hate the idea of their left hand knowing what their right hand does. Above all creeds they yet practically obey the highest of all, and do their good deeds with a shame-faced shrinking from publicity that is simply inexplicable to those whose names figure so prominently in subscription lists.

Amidst all the memories of that strenuous time, which cluster so thickly around me as I write, none are more delightful than these—of the sympathy and practical help I met with from those who were almost as poor as myself. And, be it noted, not one of these dear friends were in sympathy with the work which lay nearest my heart, the open-air preaching. They were not Christian Brothers, nor did they feel at all inclined to come under my teaching. It is,

I fear, a lurid commentary upon the way in which, within the churches, practical Christianity is followed up, that in all my extensive experience, most of the individual helping, the ready sympathy in practical ways for those in trouble has come from " unbelievers " as they are contemptuously termed. An enormous amount of " charity " is dispensed by the churches in orthodox ways with due recognition of the donors, and often more than adequate reward to the agents who distribute, but at whatever cost I must affirm that it is nothing either as regards quantity, quality, and effectiveness, with that individually given by those who make no claim upon the name of Christian at all. What does this mean ? To me it means that while the Christian says that he is unworthy of the least of the Father's mercies, he endeavours to find out before bestowing a halfpenny in charity that the recipient shall be worthy in his estimation of *his* charity ! I speak as a man, but that is my opinion.

# CHAPTER X

## THE COTTAGE *ORNÉE*

THERE must have been in the minds of those who have read so far, and who have had some practical experience themselves, a dim enquiry, how did this feeble tradesman keep out of the County Court? For to those who have ever been in a like position to mine, the terror of the County Court, the nearest approach to the Cadi under the palm tree that modern jurisprudence can know, has been ever present. It is true that after I became unable to pay my wholesale purveyor's bills as they came in, I was put to great straits in writing, requesting, yes, begging, for time to pay for what I had bought, because I had not yet sold it, nor indeed had I any hope of doing so. These, however, were not the people to sue me in a small debts court. Nor since I never had credit from the neighbouring shopkeepers had I any difficulty with them, poor people, whose only remedy, and that a weak one, with rogues lay in the County Court.

Thus it came about that I only knew the charming little one-story building in the Camberwell New Road, which some delightful writer, I forget who, has characterised as the " Cottage Ornée," by sight, and its inscription, cut into the stucco of its façade, " Lambeth County Court," never gave me a qualm. Every day I passed it either on foot or, when I was well to do, on the twenty-four a shilling tram, which ran from Camberwell Green to Vauxhall Station, and it really never occurred to me that one day I should be all too familiar with the precincts. That day came, however, and in a peculiar manner. I had hinted that I was on none too good terms with my landlord, who lived next door be it remembered, and our closer acquaintance did not at all improve our relations. The fact is, I suppose, that he never understood me, and I am sure I never understood him. He was trying to make a living out of his shop next door and the little property which I rented from him, and resented any attempts I made to compel him to render my premises more habitable. I naturally saw things from my own standpoint, and reprobated him for a soulless despot, who, having secured me as a lessee of his rotten, tumble-down premises, expected me, while paying him a heavy rental, to keep them in repair, which I resented accordingly; and at last matters came to the pitch of my refusing to pay any more rent until that desirable messuage, which I was lessee of, should have its roof repaired and made tenantable, as I put it, for human beings.

He did not see eye to eye with me, and fell back

upon the landlord's best friend, a bum-bailiff, called in our vernacular, with every inflection of emphasis that dislike could suggest, "th' bum." A most un-enviable occupation, and one requiring a front of brass, as well as a great deal of callous energy. Such men should have no feelings, and usually appear as if they had none, for they are willing for a considera-tion that all the odium incurred by the landlord should be transferred to them. There are, of course, exceptions to this general rule, for some bailiffs are kindly and generous and honest, but I unfortunately came across a bad specimen of the genus indeed. He entered my shop one day, during my absence, and enquired for me, well knowing that I was away at the Office, and gradually wormed his way into the confidence of my wife by representing himself to her as a friend who was deeply interested in my welfare, and anxious to arrange amicably the little difference, as he put it, between my landlord and myself. She was quite won by his manner, and entertained him with tea until my arrival, when she introduced him to me in his assumed character.

I was quite as easily gulled as she was, and after a few minutes amicable conversation, during which he repeatedly professed to be able to smooth matters between my landlord and myself, as it was so undesir-able that neighbours such as we were should be on bad terms, I showed him over the house, and pointed out to him its deplorable condition. In this connection

I also mentioned my many difficulties, and the impossibility of my undertaking the necessary repairs even if I felt disposed to, which I most emphatically did not. This confidence of mine corroborated what my wife had been telling him, though that I did not then know, and should have made him sorry for the task he had set himself. But presently, to my amazement, he said, quite casually, "Well, about this quarter's rent, don't you think you'd better pay it and save trouble?" I stared at him for a moment, not even then realising that I had been entertaining a wolf in sheep's clothing, and then replied, "I couldn't pay it anyhow before the end of the month" (it was then about the twentieth), "but I shan't pay it until he makes the place fit to live in."

"Oh well," he answered coolly, "you know your own business best, I suppose. I've done all I can, and if you won't pay, I must leave a man in possession, that's all. He's waiting outside. There's my card," and with that he displayed to my horror-stricken gaze a piece of pasteboard on which the words, "Broker and Appraiser" stood out apparently in letters of fire. My eyes were opened indeed, but it was too late. I could only promise to do what I could on the morrow, and plead that in the meantime he would keep his man off the premises, in view of the harm in a business sense it would undoubtedly do me. This, after much apparent cogitation and very grudgingly, he consented to do on my solemn promise to have the money there for him, with his fee in addition, the next evening at six o'clock. And then he strode out with the air of a conqueror, all his suavity of demeanour having vanished with the necessity for it.

Eight pounds to be obtained by six o'clock the next day! No credit anywhere, not a bit of portable property pawnable, and pay-day ten days off. Yes, I know what you are thinking, reader, " Is it possible that this man had let his rent fall due without making any provision for it ? " To go into explanations would take far too long, and would, besides, not be over profitable, so the easiest way is to say that I *had* been so foolish and improvident, and whatever other epithet may be chosen, and not for the first time either. But hitherto I had always managed to pay up well within the usual days of grace allowed without having a bailiff presented to me.

I'm afraid I did not get much sleep that night, which was unusual, for although I did not sleep long I slept soundly as a rule. One fact stood out prominently in my memory, the advertisement of a philanthropist in one of the streets off the Adelphi, who was always prepared to advance to gentlemen in permanent employment, who might be temporarily embarrassed, £5 on their simple note of hand without any bothering security whatever. Prudence whispered, " Don't do it." Necessity growled, " You must." And so next day, during my luncheon hour, I hurried with a thumping heart to the address given in the advertisement. The matter was simplicity itself. The gentleman was a well-fed young Hebrew of quiet manners, who merely asked me a civil question or two and referred to a red book. " All right, Mr Bullen, you can have £5 on your signing this promissory note to pay £5. 10s. this day month." I accepted eagerly, shook hands cordially, and in two minutes was speeding back to the office with this precious fiver in my pocket. The making up of the other £3 was a matter of much more difficulty, and I am not justified in giving details, but I hurried home at five with £7. 19s. 6d. in my pocket, and a feeling of ability to face anybody and anything.

But had I known it, I had just taken a step that cost me afterwards more suffering than I even now care to think of. That simple little fiver, so easily borrowed at 120 per cent. per annum, and parted with directly to pay a debt that ought never to have become a debt ! Well, I cannot say that it the was beginning of sorrows, but it certainly was the beginning of a great accession to the sorrows I already had. And I went home as glad as a boy who had just passed his first examination, as pleased as if I had just found five pounds instead of having added some rivets to the chain already round my neck.

The broker was waiting for me when I got home— when I saw him I felt with a chill that he knew all

K.

that I had been doing to get his claim settled—and I greeted him manfully, but without effusion, lugging the money out of my pocket and pushing it over towards him. He counted it in silence and gave me a receipt, and then said, as if it was an after-thought, " Oh, a friend of mine asked me to give you this as I should be seeing you." *This* was a summons to the Lambeth County Court to give reasons why I should not summarily pay an account of £7 odd incurred for attendance and medicine some five months before. What I thought as I gazed at the document I do not know, what I said were the banal words " All right, I'll attend to it." Yes *I* could attend to it, returnable in a week's time too. My pay of £9. 3s. 4d. never seemed to go very far in the settling of the demands made upon me, but this month it seemed as if it were a mere farce to take it up at all, so little would it do. And then there were the poor rates, the gas account, the water rate, and a few other little things of that kind, to say nothing of the perfectly ridiculous yet nevertheless imperative necessity of obtaining food for six persons.

However, as long as the demands were not made on the spur of the moment, as it were, I felt, like the immortal Micawber, that something might turn up, and so I went stolidly on my way, only carefully noting the date of my enforced appearance at the County Court. My chief difficulty at this troublous time, as it always was afterwards while I was a shopkeeper, was the absence of ready money, even in such small amounts as might suffice to pay the few pence required to pay my fare to and from the office on a wet day. This gave an exquisite relish to the farce of receiving not merely begging circulars, but visits of calling beggars, whether they boldly asked alms, or in a confidential manner requested the loan of a few shillings for a fortnight.

When the day of my appearance at Court arrived, I was punctual in my attendance, having obtained a day's leave from the office, and I must admit, that in spite of the urgency of my own private affair, I found it possible to take a great amount of interest, and find a great deal of amusement in what was gonig on. I must also confess that I was really appalled at the utter disregard of the value of the oath taken by those appearing as plaintiffs or defendants. It was rare, indeed, to find in any case that the plaintiff did not swear one thing and the defendant the exact opposite. The duty of the Registrar (I had not made the acquaintance of the judge yet) seemed to consist of deciding which was the most likely story out of each pair told him, and acting accordingly. And as I was not called upon till midday, I heard a great deal of this, so much indeed that I felt full of wonder how any man could occupy such a position as that presiding officer did and retain any belief in what anybody said.

At last my case was called, and it was simplicity

itself. " Do you owe this money ? " queried the Registrar sharply. " Yes, sir," I replied. " Then why don't you pay it ? " was the next and most obvious question. " Because I can't," I answered humbly, and was proceeding to explain those reasons, although I could see the gentleman I was addressing was taking no notice of me, when he suddenly stopped me and called upon my creditor (who I may say, was not the doctor, but an agent to whom the doctor paid a percentage for collecting his debts) to give evidence of my means. He stated what he knew very fairly, viz. that I kept a shop and had a permanent situation. Upon which the Registrar ordered me to pay within a fortnight and called the next case. I was, of course, mightily astonished at being so peremptorily silenced, especially as I felt sure that from what I had seen that morning I should have got on much better had I denied the debt altogether. But I was only then commencing my acquaintance with our laws, as affecting debtor and creditor, wherein at every turn a premium is placed upon dishonesty and falsehood, and the honest debtor seldom obtains either justice or mercy. Of that, however, later on.

That first experience of mine at the County Court, apart altogether from my personal interest in it, was a serious revelation to me. I had no idea before how futile were the oath-takings, with what lightness of heart men and women perjured themselves. I do not mean by that any reference to difficulty of expression or treachery of memory, but deliberate lying upon oath, and that too about such trivial matters as a few shillings, or even, as it appeared to me, for the sake of preventing a friend from losing a case. Also I was amazed to see how lightly this matter was regarded by the officials; for I had always looked upon perjury as a crime of such magnitude as to be even spoken of with bated breath. But these officials lived in an atmosphere of perjury, and had I suppose, grown case hardened, at anyrate, they heard it all day long and took no heed as far as I could see. I make no excuse for referring to this matter again, because of what I believe to be its tremendous significance.

Another thing in which I then first became much interested was the ease with which anybody possessed of sufficient impudence and plausibility could accumulate debt, repudiate it or ignore it, or delay paying any part of it until summoned for it, and then quite easily, as it appeared to me, get off by paying a ridiculous sum per month. Here in many cases I failed to see any justice at all. To illustrate my meaning I will quote two typical cases. The first was that of a man who did not appear himself, but sent his young wife, who was rather good-looking, very smartly dressed, and completely equipped with saucy self-confidence and much power of repartee. The debt was £15 for meat supplied from day to day.

Small amounts had been paid off the ever-growing bill, but at last the butcher, who was in a very small way of business, feeling that his hopes of ever getting his money were growing so faint as almost to disappear altogether, summoned the debtor for the amount. Undoubtedly he had been very patient, but then if such patience were not common among small traders, however would the poor live ?

The debt was not denied, for a wonder, but the lady pleaded, " My 'usban's ben aht o' work fur a good many weeks, an' he aint earnin' more'n fifteen shillin' a week nah, me washup, an' so we cahn't pye this money." " But you have been still running up the bill," said the judge. " Yus me washup," said the lady, " we 'ad ter live, yer see." Upon being appealed to for leniency to the debtor under these sad conditions, the butcher successfully proved that the consumer of his meat had four carts and six horses, and kept four men in constant employment. As to being ill or out of work, these statements were pure embroidery, the whole concern was in flourishing order, and had been for years. The butcher wound up by declaiming indignantly, " An' I gotter find a bloke like that in grub wot I gotter pye my hard-earned brass down on the nail fer, 'im as could buy an' sell me twicet over any dye ? " it did seem queer.

But the net result was that the debtor was condemned to pay his debt of £15 and costs off at the rate of *five shillings* per month, and the lady danced out of the witness box with a *moue* full of derision at the hapless butcher. Lest this may seem to be an especially chosen incident I here assert that such a case is peculiarly common and typical as is the next case I quote, but the reason for the difference in treatment I leave wiser heads than mine to determine.

A pale, slender man neatly dressed and giving his occupation as that of a clerk, was summoned by a doctor for a debt and costs of £5. 10s. This, by the way, was at another County Court and before a judge. Asked why he did not pay the bill, the defendant pleaded that the amount originally asked was excessive, inasmuch as it was for three visits and two bottles of medicine. He further stated that he was just emerging from a long period of unemployment, and that his wages were now £2 per week.

Without calling upon the doctor the judge thundered at the unfortunate debtor " who are you to assess the value of the doctor's services ? " Pay the whole amount within a fortnight. That'll do, I won't hear another word. Next case." And the hapless debtor went slowly down and out as much surprised as I was, doubtless, at the strange inequalities of justice. The case was peculiarly noticeable in that the defendant, having moved a long way from the neighbourhood after incurring the debt, had voluntarily returned to the doctor with the first money he had earned to pay his bill, and only refused on account of what he considered its exorbitant amount. I make no comment, I only wonder.

Now came for a time a blessed relief, not that is from any of the major burdens, but from my most pressing necessities. Orders flowed in from all quarters, and I found the utmost difficulty in keeping pace with them. I used to get up at half-past two or three in the morning, and after making myself a cup of tea get to work with such furious energy, that I look back upon it now with utter amazement. Many and many a time I have done what anybody might consider a really good day's work before breakfast-*time* (I never had any breakfast) or say eight o'clock, when I must needs wash and dress and rush off to my office work where I was due at nine. By the time one o'clock came, I had a decent appetite which I stayed very cheaply, my early experience now standing me in good stead. A half-penny loaf, a pennyworth of cheese, a half-penny beetroot or a penny tomato with a half a pint of mother-in-law (stout and bitter) to wash it down with, used to make me a very good meal at a cost of threepence or four-pence. Or I would, if flush of money, have a quarter of boiled pork and a ha'porth of pease pudding, which with a halfpenny loaf or a ha'porth of potatoes made a sumptuous meal and one that I enjoyed far more than any elaborate banquets I have ever attended since.   And the total cost never exceeded sixpence.

Such meals had a relish all their own, and if business drove me to a cook-shop for the orthodox cut off the joint and two vegetables for sixpence, I never enjoyed it as well, with one exception.   A local cook-shop made a speciality of stewed steak, at least that is what they called it, though it was really shin of beef, and it was very good and satisfying, with plenty of thick brown gravy.   They only charged fourpence for it, so that with a pennyworth of potatoes and a pennyworth of pudding afterwards I could make a really good meal for sixpence.   Here I learned what was of great use to me, a lesson that I now see inculcated on every hand, how small a quantity of food the body really needs to do good work upon, and conversely how much more food than is really necessary the average man or woman does consume.   But I cannot take any credit for this learning, for like so many other useful lessons conveyed to us it was compulsory, I had no choice but to learn it.   The result has been at any rate that the " pleasures of the table " have never since then meant anything to me, one plain meal in the middle of the day sufficing for all my needs, and keeping me in such health as the results of my overwork will allow me.

Still I should be very sorry to go about endeavouring to force other people to go and do likewise, because I have learned very thoroughly how great a factor is individuality, and how true is the old proverb that one man's meat is another man's poison. And I humbly think that if some of our vociferous propagandists would learn that lesson also it would be much better for the general peace.

# CHAPTER XI

## NEARING THE END

THERE was no especial reason as far as I know for closing that last chapter, and commencing a new one, except that it was getting too long in my opinion. For the story I was telling was incomplete, I having gone off at an unexpected angle on the question of food supplies. However, I will now resume and say that the influx of work I mentioned lasted for a fortnight, during the whole of which time I can aver that, except on Sundays, I was never in bed after 3 a.m. or before 11 p.m., and that I was often so weary on coming home from the city with a load of moulding, that I would sit down on a chair in the shop and be unable to rise for half an hour. But as I would not allow myself to think about the future, or ask myself what was the good of it all, I was not unhappy, and I was able to take a good deal of pride in my work. And by the time the pressure slackened, I had settled that wretched summons, had paid my rates, and a few other immediate liabilities, besides being able to buy a few sorely needed articles of clothing for the family.

There was however no lightening of the old burden of debt, and in fact I realised that nothing short of a miracle would enable me to do that. For if I got all the work I craved for I should surely break down, while the utmost that I could earn would not do much more than pay the heavy current expenses of the shop. Had I been able to employ some help, it might have been better, but I don't know about that. I had to do my own errands—I could not delegate my buying in the city to anybody else, although it did entail such a heavy burden upon me physically. Meanwhile I paid cash for everything I had, though I did not pay anything of the bills already incurred.

In this connection I have an amusing recollection. The moulding merchant with whom I dealt was an elderly German in a large way of business, and I had always heard of him as a kindly old soul, but had never come into personal contact with him. Now, however, I owed him nearly £30, for which I had given a bill, and was constantly renewing it; and, consequently, although I dealt with the firm for all my mouldings, and paid cash, I dreaded meeting one of the principals, and indeed slank in and out of the premises like a thief. One day, however, I ran right into the old gentleman, who looked at me keenly and said, " Ach, Meesder Boollen, aindt id ? " I humbly answered, " Yes, sir." " Yes, sir," he rather mockingly replied, " now I haf peen in pizness here in London for more as tirty year, andt I nefer ad a gustomer dot righdt me sooch nice ledders as you. But you tondt send me no money, hein ? I likes to read dose ledders, dey vas very goot, but vy tondt you pay some money too, hein ? "

I endeavoured to give him such reasons as I had, and he listened carefully, saying when I had done, " Ach so ! Vell, you pay ven you can, undt tondt you go puying your mouldings someveres ellas mit your ready money. Ve all haf droubles, undt ve get over 'em. You get over yours somedime I hope, and den you pay your bill. Goodt efening." And he turned and went into his office, while I went on into the moulding shop with a warm feeling of gratitude to the kind old man, and a firm determination that he should not suffer loss through me if I could possibly help it.

Thenceforward I struggled on, sometimes feeling as if the waters which were always about my chin would suddenly submerge me, but compelled to go on. I often compared myself at this time to a man running in front of a train, between two high walls, allowing of no escape to either side, having no choice but to run or be run over. Still I found solace in my books and newspapers, and relieved my mind of some of its cares by taking an intense interest in political matters as well as the open air propaganda of religion.

What I suppose will strike some people with amazement is the fact that starting as an extreme radical, never a Home Ruler, I gradually became utterly disgusted with the radical position. Full of admiration for the socialism of Christ, I grew to detest the socialism that I saw being practised by the noisy party in the vestry, and the doctrines I heard preached by the socialists in the open air simply filled me with dismay. For it was nothing else but the survival of the unfit and incurably idle, the morally degenerate, at the expense of the fit, the hard-working and ever-striving classes, an effort in short not to level up, but to level down, a complete subversion of the golden rule of do to all men as ye would they should do unto you. Get all you can for yourself, and the devil take anybody else. Eat and drink all you can at somebody else's expense, no matter who. Beget as many children as you like, and let somebody else care for them. And so on. Oh! it used to make me very sick and sorry, but I am glad to say that in my preaching of what I felt to be right, I always had a most sympathetic and respectful hearing; and I really do believe that the detestable doctrines of loaferdom and savagery which masquerade as socialism have very little hold upon the ordinary people of our streets.

Another great solace of mine was an occasional chat with my fellow shopkeepers, most of whom, like myself, had a severe struggle to live. It makes me positively ill to hear the blatant cant that is talked about the working man, meaning journeymen and labourers only. The small London surburban shopkeeper toils far harder than any of them, is preyed upon by them to an extent which must be incredible to those who don't know, is taxed almost out of existence to support them in the schemes continually being propounded for their benefit by their representatives on the Borough Councils, and is quoted in radical newspapers as the bitter enemy of the working classes.

I found them a kindly, genial, well-informed class of men, shrewd and keen, as indeed they need be in order to live, and particularly free from the petty vices of public-house loafing, betting, and bad language, which are so peculiarly the characteristics of the " working man." But the hardest hit of them all I think were the small grocers. I knew two or three of them intimately, men whose lives were one long grey grind of labour. Who could not live unless they opened very early in the morning, before the big capitalist shops, such as the Home and Colonial, Lipton's, etc., and kept open late at night for the same reason. Even then they would not have been able to live but for giving credit, which the big combinations do not allow their employees to do. Many hundreds of families would come to the workhouse long before they do, especially in hard winters, but for these small tradesmen giving them credit for the bare necessities of life, and thus tiding them over the pinching time. This system of first aid can hardly be called philanthropy, since those who extend it do it for a living, and yet in the multitudinous life of poor London it is a huge and most important factor. Even the poor itinerant coal merchant, who goes to the wharf and buys his coal by the ton, and then retails it through the streets in small quantities from dawn to dark, may be seen on Saturdays, the hardest day of all, when his selling of coal is done, painfully dragging his weary way from door to door, collecting the payment for the coal he has been vending on credit all the week.

The costermonger, who has a regular pitch and regular customers, competing with the tradesmen to whom he stands opposite in the most unfair way, in that he has no rent, rates, or taxes to pay, will give credit, and generously too, although he may often through a bad week have to pay usurious interest in order to borrow the money to go to market with. In fact all the small traders give credit, for the reasons I have already stated. Of course, in this way much very inferior stuff is got rid of, because it is certain that he who buys on credit retail with either tradesman will have to pay higher prices than for cash, or will have to put up with inferior goods, since it is impossible to scrutinise too closely what you are receiving on credit unless indeed you are of sufficient rank to make a tradesman glad to serve you on any terms.

One great exception to the universal rule of credit is the publican. Because his wares are a luxury, and the indulgence in them in many cases prevents the payment of legitimate claims, money can always be found for him much, to the other shopkeepers' disgust. So far is this system of credit carried out that I have known men get their ha'penny morning and evening paper on credit, and even take their workman's ticket, which their news vendor kept a supply of for the convenience of customers, with the casual remark, "Stony broke this mornin', old man, pay you on Saturday." More fools they to allow it, I hear some folks say, but such poor traders allow a good many things to be done to them rather than get the name of being close-fisted with their customers.

To return for a moment to the work of the small shopkeeper, take for instance the butcher. He must needs go to market, no matter what the weather may be, as early as three or four in the morning; he is hard at work all day fully exposed to the weather, and on Saturday must keep open until one o'clock on Sunday morning. In addition to this in many neighbourhoods it is imperative for him to open again on Sunday for a few hours in order to satisfy the demands of those curious folk who will not do their marketing on Saturday while the " houses " (public understood) are open, and when they close at twelve o'clock are unfit for anything but quarrelling or reeling home to bed. Hence Sunday trading with all its attendant evils and its cruel strain upon the small tradesman.

I must confess, however, that although I sympathised

L

so deeply with all my shopkeeping associates, personally, I did not suffer as they did. For my business being of a non-essential character it did not greatly matter how late I opened my shop or how early I closed it. That I had to carry my materials home from the city was due to the facts of my position being so bad that I could not lay in a stock, and partly because I found it cheaper and more convenient, if more laborious, to buy my moulding as I got orders for frames. Another thing I must say in justice to my customers, and in spite of the reputation of the neighbourhood as impressed upon me when I started in business there—I made practically no bad debts. Perhaps that was partly due to the fact that people do not, in humble walks of life that is, have pictures framed until they have the money ready to pay for the work; and another thing, when I took work home, I always waited for the money, for I always wanted it urgently.

Occasionally, it is true, I had a little difficulty with people who talked grandiloquently of calling round in a day or two, and paying a bill of a few shillings, or of sending a cheque, say, of seven and sixpence, but they were exceedingly seldom. But I had many heart burnings through the vagaries of a certain type of person who would come in and waste hours of my time (and I noticed that these visits usually occurred when I was urgently busy) examining mouldings and getting estimates up to several pounds in value.

After which they vanished, and I never saw them again.

Once I was fairly victimised, though fortunately for only a small amount, but I must plead that it took a long time. And as the story is, in my opinion at any rate, exceedingly romantic, I may be pardoned for telling it at length. In the course of business we had made the acquaintance of a French lady, said to be a countess, and through her we became intimate with her son and a lady from Sweden reputed to be his wife. He was a pupil of Schubert, and an exquisite violinist, and as I was always a great lover of music, and he was exceedingly hospitable, we often went to his house, which was close at hand in Melbourne Grove. There we met a truculent individual, black-avised, as the old description runs, speaking a most hideous travesty of English, and withal behaving as if he owned the establishment. His name I never rightly knew, but it was nearly all consonants I remember, and he was introduced to me as a Russian prince who had taken a prominent part in the tragedy of Plevna, and held the rank of Captain in the Preobrajensky Guards. Only a day or two elapsed after my first meeting with this warrior when he appeared in my shop, and endeavoured to tell me a wonderful tale of a diamond necklace worth some thousands of pounds, the property of a French lady of high rank. This splendid article had been pawned for a large sum, and the ticket had nearly run out, but if it were redeemed it could be repledged for a greatly increased sum, and the kindly person who would advance the cash for this transaction would make something like 200 per cent. for his amiability. How I understood all this I do not know but I did, and smiled sardonically at the idea of me being selected for the operation, *me*! who never had any money except what I was in immediate and pressing need of.

His highness seemed genuinely and pathetically surprised, also somewhat incredulous, when I managed to convey to him the true state of affairs concerning myself. I did not, however, trouble to tell him that I felt absolutely bristling with caution towards him, regarding him as the worst type of the *Chevalier d'industrie* I had ever heard of. So he went away, but did not cease his visits to me, sometimes flashing a pocketful of gold, sometimes without a sou. At last he made his grand coup. He advertised in the French papers for a valet to attend upon a Russian nobleman, who, as he had much valuable jewellery, would require a deposit of £70 as security against dishonesty. Then he took a house in East Dulwich Grove on a twenty-one year lease, and entered into negotiations with a furnishing company to fit it up. Of course he got his valet and his security, with part of which he paid the first instalment of the purchase of his furniture. Within a week he had sold every item of that furniture, and leaving his hapless valet to starve in the empty house, had departed to the wilds of Soho to lead a gay life as long as the money lasted. For this was his peculiarity, stamping him indubitably as one of the *boys* so graphically depicted by Mr Ernest Binstead ; he would lie, swindle, steal, do anything to obtain money, sell the bed from under his dying mother, let us say, or worse than that if it were possible, and when the money was in his possession he would fling it broadcast with both hands as if he were lord of millions.

He had hardly disappeared before a man came to me who gave me his card, which described him as a diamond merchant. He told me a pitiful story of how the vanished nobleman had victimised him in the matter of a diamond necklace, at which I felt the corners of my mouth relax as I thought " same old song and dance." In consequence of the evil wrought in his accounts by this most untoward transaction, he was under the painful necessity of raising a loan on a bill of sale. His house was fairly well furnished, but—he had no pictures. Now I knew what pictures were to a house and—by the way—what a beautiful lot of engravings I had framed to be sure. (I almost purred.) If I would only lend him a few just to hang on his walls while the money-lender looked around, he would be glad to pay me a pound for the accommodation, and I could have the pictures back the next morning. Of course I wanted a pound very badly, and I didn't see much risk, and the pictures had been in stock so long that I didn't reckon them at more than £2, 10s. anyhow, so I said, " All right, I'll bring them round in an hour's time." He thanked me and left. He had not been gone more than five minutes, when a neighbour who was a baker came in and asked me if that wasn't the tenant of No. — East Dulwich Grove, who had just gone out. I said it was, and gave an outline of the transaction just completed. My neighbour quietly said that they owed him fifty bob for bread, and he meant to have it, and left.

I took the pictures up and hung them. They looked very well, and the family was loud in expressions of admiration. After many assurances that I should have them back the next day, I left, meeting on my way back my baker neighbour. He called on me about two hours later, saying that he'd got his money, but only after kicking up such a row that the respectable Grove was quite scandalised, and even the paupers at the workhouse infirmary opposite were interested. I only smiled, for I thought I understood. When, however, I found an my arrival home next day that my pictures had *not* been returned, and on calling round at the house found it empty, I realised that in spite of all my confidence in my own astuteness I had been done. Two days later, I saw my pictures exposed for sale in a local pawnshop at a far higher price than I had ever dared to ask for them. I had a chat with the pawnbroker on the subject, and he seemed very much amused. I found it difficult to understand why then, although it is clearer to me now.

I also had a visit once from a certain notorious adventuress, whose alias was, I believe, Mrs Gordon. She made quite a lot of interesting copy for the newspapers about that time, and her picture was published in various journals. But her plan for getting something out of me was not very ingenious, at any rate I easily evaded it, and took considerable credit to myself for my cleverness in doing so.

Taking things all round, however, I was very fortunate in not being victimised to any extent, for there is a large number of ingenious folk going about London whose business it is to entrap unwary tradesmen who deal in goods which may be easily disposed of for a trifle of ready money. Dealers in perishable commodities, such as butchers, bakers, grocers, or green-grocers, are tolerably safe from the attentions of these gentry, but jewellers, furniture dealers, picture dealers, etc., are particularly liable to be preyed upon, as I found, and indeed my poverty was several times my only protection. I could not fall into their traps, because I wanted money on account, which they never had.

Now, strange as it may seem, I really did build up a fairly good reputation in the neighbourhood as a picture-framer of taste and punctuality, but owing to the fact that I could not wait upon customers at all hours, could not, that is, attend to both businesses at once, I was unable to do well. And then there is for suburban picture-framers a distinctly slack season which extends from June until November. Then when people are saving for their holidays, enjoying them or recovering from them, the poor maker of frames may as well close his shop unless he has other strings to his bow. The expenses still go on, rent must be paid, gas bills met, etc., but my takings averaged five shillings a week.

At one of these periods, having received an invitation from a distant relative in the wilds of Wiltshire to spend a fortnight down there at an inclusive cost which was less than I must have spent had I remained at home, I decided to go away. On leaving I pasted a notice on the shutters : " Gone for a much needed holiday, return on the 25th of August.—F. T. Bullen." When I did return, I was greeted by all my shopkeeping neighbours with sardonic surprise, not unmixed with scorn. They all said they never thought to see me again, having fully expected that I had " done a guy," as they inelegantly put it, and several hinted rather plainly that they considered me a fool for ever coming back ; which went to show very clearly that they knew as well as I did myself that I was in difficulties. Indeed in a small community such as ours was, it was not possible to conceal one's straits any more than it would be in a little country town. I have no doubt that every one of my neighbours knew how few were the customers that came into my shop as well as they knew what the expenses of the shop were, in fact, as they put it frequently to one another, I kept the shop, the shop didn't keep me.

Yes, everything seemed to trend downwards towards a place of the depth of which I had no conception. Every fresh run of orders at the rare intervals when they did arrive, only seemed to stave off the evil day which would surely come, and it is not putting the matter one whit too strongly to say that I had lost all hope of ever doing any good for myself and family. Neither did I see how I was going to get rid of what had come to be a perfectly diabolical burden, the shop. Despite all my efforts I got deeper and deeper into debt, and among other things the crushing load of the rates, then going up by leaps and bounds, owing to the socialistic tendency of the local authorities, made me feel peculiarly bitter; especially when I saw the troops of able-bodied men slouching about the workhouse recreation grounds.

# CHAPTER XII

## TOWARDS CAREY STREET

A KEEN sense of humour is one of my richest blessings, one that I prize more than I can tell, but never before have I felt so keenly the great desirability of being able to express myself humorously in writing. For this narrative of mine, drab in all its essentials, tends ever to more gloom. There were touches of humour in my life, for I know that I often had a hearty laugh, but I remember too that this healthful exercise was usually after I had gone to bed, and was reading one of my favourite books for perhaps the twentieth time. But I am bound to say that any relief to the gloom of my daily life except on Sundays, the delights of which I have spoken before, was almost entirely wanting. I could, I dare say, introduce a few humorous touches occasionally, for which the reader would be duly grateful, but it would be at the expense of truth, and anyhow it would be of a saturnine character if it were drawn from my experience of every day life.

Take, for instance, a scene which I witnessed on Saturday night late, outside the East Dulwich Hotel, at the corner of Goose Green. It had been raining for a long time, and the streets were in an exceedingly bad state. Just there, however, some attempt had been made earlier in the day to sweep them, and in consequence the kennel on both sides was full of liquid mud, had become in fact a creek of mud a yard wide and several inches deep. I was taking some pictures home during a slight break in the weather, and rounding this corner I saw two men, both of whom were drunk, amicably endeavouring to take one another home. They staggered about a good deal, getting nearer and nearer the kerb, until one of them slipped down, and the other, endeavouring to raise him, rolled over on the top of him. Locked in a close embrace, and making no sound, they rolled into the kennel; while I, the solitary spectator, helpless by reason of my burden, became doubly so because of a perfect agony of laughter. Like hippopotami they wallowed in the viscid stream, and at last emerged on the farther side, as Mrs Gamp would say, a marks of mud, but still horizontal. They rolled right across the road, which was fairly wide, and into the creek of mud on the other side where, with their heads on the kerb, they rested from their arduous journey apparently full of peace. A policeman and a little knot of spectators had by this time arrived, and much discussion, punctuated with shouts of laughter, went on as to what should be done with and for them. What was done eventually I do not know, for I had to fulfil my errand, aching all over with my paroxysms of laughter. Yet as the boys say when they are the victims, " I don't see anything to laugh at."

This digression is of malice aforethought, because I cannot help feeling that readers will say " I wish Bullen wouldn't so persistently sue for our sympathy. Surely he must have had some good times." And that is the worst of the simple annals of the poor ; they are deeply interesting of course to the protagonists, but are apt to become wearisome in the recital, because, as the Irishman said of his wife, they are all worse and no better. However I went on, doggedly, hopelessly, not because I was a brave man struggling with adversity, but because as far as my limited intelligence went I couldn't do anything else. Several people, one of whom most generously helped me over a tremendously difficult stile, suggested bankruptcy as being the obvious way out of all my troubles, but that I felt was impossible. True, I *was* a bankrupt *de facto* but not *de jure*, and I believed that if I did become a bankrupt in law, I should lose my last hope of earning a living, my job at the office. So I ruled that suggestion out as impracticable, for supposing I did lose my job, it was no figure of speech to call it my last hope. I was rapidly nearing forty, my own profession was irrevocably closed to me even if the state of my health would have allowed me to take it up again, and as for my other employment, with thousands of abler, younger men clamouring for it, what possible prospect had I ? and I had a wife and five young children ! I will not say that I was absolutely friendless, but the two or three faithful friends I had were powerless to help me except in a desperate emergency, and at a great personal sacrifice then. As a dear friend said to me the other day, while we were discussing the condition of a mutual friend who had become the victim of a most serious misfortune absolutely without fault of his own : " There is nothing more heart-breaking than to have a friend who is what the Spaniards call *gastados*, used up, no more good in this pushing world. You can't keep him, you can't ask anybody else to keep him, and in spite of yourself, with the best will in the world, you get tired of his incessant appeals for help, however piteous and sincere."

Is that not so ? and all the more sad when it is the result of misfortune and not of indolence or vice. However I did not allow myself to think, for fear I should lose my power of sleep, which I knew would be fatal. I dared not open my letters, the postman's knock sent a clutching pang through the pit of my stomach, and if it had not been for my Sundays, with their entire switch off from the terrors of every day life, I feel sure I should have gone mad. It was at this juncture that I began to write. Leaning over the counter in the empty shop I covered page after page with neat clerkly script, an exercise I always

loved, narrating my early experiences at sea. It
was a delightful relief, and as such I enjoyed it, but
if I ever had any wild dreams about publishing what
I was writing they did not last, for when I had written
about forty thousand words I put the MS. away and
forgot all about it. Finally I threw it in the dustbin,
which was a pity, for I daresay it was quite as good
as anything I have ever done in the same way since.

Meanwhile matters plodded towards that destined
end which I felt was inevitable, but would not realise.
I got into more difficulties with my landlord. The
state of the house was simply disgraceful, and he would
do nothing. Then all of us got sore throats, and the
doctor said bluntly, " It's of no use my attending you
unless you have these drains seen to ; they are a grave
danger to anybody's health who comes into your
shop ! " Thus admonished I again approached my
landlord, who sent a man to put two dabs of mortar
upon the soil-pipe at the back of the house. Then
in despair I wrote to the vestry, and very promptly
their surveyor appeared. He condemned not merely
my drains, but those of the whole row of houses in
which my house stood. And then there was a pretty
fine how d'ye do, I can tell you. My premises were
all ripped up at the back to get at the drains, which of
course were under the foundations, and when everything was in a state of chaos the operations mysteri-
ously ceased. Rats invaded the house and devoured
our small stock of provisions, until I took to hanging

them up as we used to do on board ship. I wrote piteous letters to the vestry, imploring them for mercy's sake to finish the job, but they took no notice and kept on doing so.

Then I made a bold stroke. I wrote to the Local Government Board, placing the whole facts before them. Talk about red tape and bureaucracy! Never have I dreamed of such celerity. Within forty-eight hours the work was completed, and I received from Whitehall a copy of an indignant letter from the vestry denouncing my complaint, as the work in question was done. I never before realised how efficient a public department might be in the proper hands. Those drains of mine had been open for three weeks, and there had been absolutely no response to my repeated applications to have the work done, when I took the step I have detailed.

This little affair cost my landlord (so he said) £25, a large sum for a man in his position, and this did not improve our relations, as might be supposed. But I hardly thought he would go to the length he did. It is customary for such tenants as I was to take a few days' grace for payment of the quarter's rent, which varies from one week to six according to the disposition of the landlord, and the circumstances of the tenant. Naturally I took as long as I could, and as long as I paid within a month was usually considered a good payer. With this landlord, however, I had to be very careful, especially after his last feat. Still I was not prepared to find, as I did on coming home on the evening of quarter day, three bailiffs in my humble abode. One was an emissary of the landlord's, whose rent was only due at twelve that day; one was for the inhabited house-duty, a trifling matter of a pound, including landlord's property tax; and one was from some other creditor whose claim I had overlooked. The total amount with costs of all their claims amounted to a little less than £20.

I confess that unable as I generally was to extract any fun out of my troubles, this time was an exception. As I was introduced to each of my uninvited guests in turn, and heard their claims, I was suddenly seized with the humour of the situation, and laughed until I was fain to hold on to the counter, or I should have fallen down. My wife stood at the door of the shop parlour looking most anxiously at me, for she thought, as she afterwards told me, that my brain had given way at last, while the three bums looked at me, and at one another in an undecided irresolute fashion, which only made me laugh all the more. However, I gradually recovered, and then said, " Well, gentlemen, I am sorry for you if you have decided to remain here, for I can neither feed you nor give you a shake-down. So you'll have but a poor time of it. I can't possibly get any money until to-morrow, and I am doubtful if I can get much then. However, that's not the point. Do the best you can. I've got some work to get on with," and I mounted to my workshop and started.

Before many minutes two of them decided to go home for the night, having delegated their authority to the third, who as soon as their backs were turned came up to me and said, that if I could give him a couple of shillings he would go too, he didn't want to put me to any trouble. I told him candidly I should have been glad to comply with his request, but as all the money I had was sixpence, I must forego the pleasure. He sighed, and then after exacting a promise that I would let him in next morning, departed also, leaving me free to get on with my work. He had not been gone many minutes when I heard my chum Bob's musical whistle below, and immediately he came bounding up, having heard the news across at the library of my having a house full of bums. He could only sympathise, but rejoiced to find me in such good spirits, was surprised also, but not more so than myself. He left a couple of shillings, with the desire that I would make one of my famous curries against the time he closed the library, when we would have supper together.

I readily agreed and hurried up with my job in order to get at my cookery, for indeed these little chance meals which I was in the habit of preparing, when there were funds, were exceedingly pleasant to me, to my family, and to Bob, who was a frequent sharer of them. I am afraid they bore a strong family likeness to the celebrated symposia indulged in by Mr Micawber and his family with David Copperfield

M

as only guest, but I can honestly say that I never pawned or sold any household goods to procure them, as the immortal Micawber did.   At any rate on this particular occasion I know that, thanks to Bob's two shillings, we had a gorgeous supper of curried skirt and kidney, with potatoes and rice ; the scent of which, as Bob said when coming in at 10.30, was enough to make a dead man sit up and ask for some.

His genial company and the good meal sufficed to keep the black shadow away long enough for me to get to sleep, but as soon as I awakened in the morning it was beside me with all its terrors.   In my emergency I bethought me of a certain money-lender who, upon a previous application to him, had informed me that he would willingly lend me £20 if I found a good surety, and would take repayment at the rate of £2 per month for twelve months.   I did not accept then, because I could not bring myself to ask anyone whom I knew to do anything I would not do myself, viz., become surety for another.   But now I was desperate, and I remembered an acquaintance who, though his salary was good, was for some reason or another chronically hard up.   He, I felt sure, would be my surety if I could spare him a little of the loan.   Utterly immoral, even dishonest and without excuse, of course, and I am going to offer none—I only set down the facts.

Upon broaching the matter to him, I found him not only willing but eager, for he himself was in urgent need of £3, and I could spare him that out of £25, the amount I proposed borrowing. So at lunch-time we sallied forth, finding our, what shall I call him, banker? in, and ready to oblige. Indeed it was fatally easy, and I was absurdly grateful, quite forgetting for the time the other gentleman in the Adelphi to whom I had to pay £1 every month as interest on a loan of £10. I handed over the £3 to my friend in need, and at five o'clock hurried home to find my three visitors ranged along the counter in the shop. In a lordly manner I paid them off, took their receipts, and we parted on the best of terms.

My amiability to the agent, however, did not extend to my landlord. I felt his behaviour to me very, very villainous, especially remembering the wretched state of the premises for which I paid him rent under his solemn agreement to keep them in habitable repair. The rain came through the roof so copiously, that I had to keep tubs up in the top rooms to prevent the whole house from becoming swamped. The ceilings were falling down, and the huge cistern supported upon brick piers in the kitchen was leaking to such an extent that it threatened daily to collapse and flood us out. So I resolved, as this was the last quarter of my three years' agreement, to remove before quarter day, and to refuse to pay him any rent, as a set off against the condition of the premises he had compelled me to live in so long.

A shop nearly opposite had become vacant by reason

of fire which had gutted the whole house, but it had been restored to its original condition, or something resembling it, and I took it. I did not blazon my intention abroad, believing that my few regular customers would easily find me, but I passed the word around among my acquaintances, and I make no doubt at all that my present landlord knew of my intentions perfectly. But he was powerless to prevent me going. Indeed, I believe that the privilege of leaving the house you hold before quarter day without fear of distraint for rent is about the only one possessed by the poor tenant, who is otherwise entirely at the mercy of his landlord. However, my landlord made no sign, while as the time approached I made all preparations for flitting. At night, after closing time, my chum Bob, to whom all violent exercises were a joy, used to come over and assist me in the transference of my goods from one house to the other, until we were fairly well fixed in the new abode, with the exception of our absolute necessaries, such as bedding, cooking utensils, etc.

On the last night, that is the 20th of the month, we worked like beavers, getting bedsteads across and put up so that the family might move in and be comfortable. Fortunately it was fine, for we had left the heaviest things, the piano and two counters, until the last. We got the two counters over without much difficulty, and then at nearly 1 a.m. we tackled the piano. We wheeled it out and along the pavement until it was opposite the new home, then lifting it into the roadway we tried to wheel it across, on its own castors of course. But it was heavy going, and in the middle of the road we stopped for breath and to wipe our brows. Suddenly a light beamed across us, and a gruff voice said, " Now then, what's this ere little game ? " We both looked up, and there stood a huge policeman, who had come up all silently in his rubber-soled boots, and was shedding the light of his bull's eye on the scene. For some idiotic reason or another, I burst into yells of laughter, Bob joined in, and the policeman followed suit. Just three idiots I suppose. But it was a quaint scene at one in the morning, in the middle of Lordship Lane.

As soon as we could speak, we explained the situation to him ; and he, bless him for a good fellow, saw it in the right light, pulled off his heavy coat, and lent a hearty hand, so that the piano was installed in the new premises in a very short time. Fortunately we had a little liquid refreshment to offer him, which he accepted in a becoming spirit, and then said, " Well, boys, I must get around before my sergeant turns up—he won't understand who I am with my coat off." And so with hearty good wishes all round we parted.

I had a busy week following, for of necessity I had to do everything that needed doing to the shop with my own hands, save what Bob did in the precious hours of his leisure after ten, which he so willingly devoted to my service. And I managed to spend a sovereign for the fascia, which was done by a man who was so drunk that he could not stand on the solid earth, but balanced himself upon a precarious plank stretched between two high trestles in front of the shop, and splashed in the letters in magnificent style. I did not watch him, for I fully expected to see him dashed to death upon the pavement at any moment; but when on his coming for his money I went out and surveyed his handiwork, I paid him without a word, for indeed there was absolutely no fault to find.

But I had hardly settled in this new shop than my troubles with regard to the building commenced, and threatened to surpass my experiences across the road. Hardly a piece of furniture could be moved upstairs without bringing some of the ceilings down, and such easily scamped places as pantries and cupboards were de-ceiled *en bloc*. The first really serious matter, however, which showed me that I had in no way bettered my position arose through the frost. I cannot fix the year properly, but it was when the frost set in some time at the end of January, and lasted until nearly June. I saw with a certain complacency my neighbours carrying water into their homes from standpipes in the streets, while my supply was intact and working well. And then with dramatic suddenness the supply-pipe from the main which ran underneath the pavement into my house burst asunder, and the water welled up through the flagstones, making a glare of ice all over the footway, which was a great danger to the passers-by.

I was immediately summoned by the Water Company on the one hand, and by the vestry on the other, to make this breakage good. With cheerful confidence I turned these demands over to my landlord, never doubting in the first place that it was his duty to repair this damage, and in the next that he would instantly perform that duty. It was a heavy blow to me when I received a curt note from him to the effect that it was no business of his, and that I could do what I chose in the matter. As if I had any choice. And so I had to call in labourers and plumbers to the tune of nearly £3, which outlay moreover did not result in my water-supply being resumed. But the shock I then received was a lasting one, for I realised that these new premises of mine bade fair to become worse than the old ones. They had been renovated after the fire by contract in the flimsiest and most casual way, and scarcely a day passed but some new defect discovered itself, until I really was afraid that the building would collapse about my ears.

Meanwhile my old landlord lost no time in putting the law's machinery in motion against me. He summoned me for two quarters' rent, one being in lieu of notice and a trifle of £10 for dilapidations caused to his premises by my neglect. Strong in my belief that I was legally justified in leaving uninhabitable premises as I did, I determined to fight, and in due time I appeared before Judge Emden at the Cottage *Ornée*. Of course I conducted my own case, and equally of course my creditor employed a solicitor. But I lost nothing by that, for I found his honour most kind and impartial. Only when I exhibited my defence explaining the condition of the premises, and asking the Judge whether I was compelled to remain in a house which was in so parlous a state, he replied in words which I can never forget : " You are not compelled to remain in such a house, you may leave before the expiration of your term, but you must pay the rent—that is the law."

Then, of course, I could only express my sorrow at having built upon so insecure a foundation, and explaining my circumstances asked for time to pay. The judge asked me what offer I could make, and I immediately said that it was impossible for me to promise more than a pound a month, which indeed it was, for at this time nearly all my office pay was eaten up by these monthly payments, and my means of living were intensely precarious. But the solicitor to the landlord in a white heat of indignation put on for the purpose, pictured me as rolling in wealth, enjoying a bloated official salary, and having a fine business in addition, so that it was the barest justice that I should be ordered to pay forthwith.

To my great joy the judge replied with sternness that he believed I had made an exceedingly fair and honest offer under the circumstances, and that if my offer were not accepted immediately he should exercise his own discretion as to what terms he should consider reasonable, and it was quite possible that he would make no order at all. This was sufficient for my opponent, one pound a month was accepted, and, as they say in the House of Lords, the matter then dropped.

# CHAPTER XIII

## COLLAPSE

IT must not be supposed that in other directions my affairs had got any smoother as time went on ; nor that, although I worked as hard as flesh and blood would permit, that I succeeded in overtaking any of my liabilities. Moreover, I began to receive unmistakable warnings that my physical capacity was becoming unequal to the constant strain I put upon it, although I only knew that my morning cough was more exhausting than it had been, and that I always awoke in the morning feeling dreadfully tired, much more so indeed than when I went to bed. And always I found myself unable to keep up those terribly punctual monthly payments, and trying to discriminate between people who would be put off and people who wouldn't.

The first immediately unpleasant result of this discrimination or attempted preference was in connection with my latter loan. Now please understand that I am bringing no indictment against the money-lender, or mean anything opprobrious in speaking of him in that way. If he had lent me thousands instead of single pounds, he would have been a banker, and if I had wanted his money for speculation instead of to pay my rent and get my family food, I should have been a financier to be esteemed instead of being a borrower to be despised. I am only, however, concerned with the plain facts now, and they are that I sent a polite letter of apology to the money-lender, telling him that—oh well, you can imagine the kind of things a defaulting debtor would say—but the whole comprising just an ordinary letter of excuse for non-payment.

To this effusion I received no reply whatever, but two days afterwards my surety came rushing to me in a state of great agitation, flourishing a telegram which he had just received from his wife, to the effect that a man had been put in possession of their furniture in default of my payment of an instalment of the loan. Desperately he demanded of me what I meant by such behaviour, and tearfully assured me that such an experience had never been his before, in which I have reason to believe he was not within the parallel lines of fact. I was as stunned as he, and promised every reparation in my power, while I knew that nothing short of that instalment would avail. So I immediately obtained leave of absence, and went a-borrowing, a frequent exercise alas, but one which I never practised without a sense of poignant shame, preventing me from degenerating into the common species of " earbiter," as he is vulgarly called, of the Montague Tigg type.

Miraculously, as I think, I succeeded in borrowing the £3 required, on my faithful promise to repay at the end of the month, from a man who was as poor as I, but more methodical, and had put it away towards his rent. Let me say before I go any further, that I did not abuse his trust, nor did I ever do so to anybody except in the single case of my surety, which I was now engaged in repairing. I hope I do not put this forward in a spirit of offensive or aggressive virtue, but I do want to disavow any association with that rotten type of man who will promise anything to get your money, will, having got it, squander it, and then ridicule you for being such a fool as to lend to him, of all people in the world. This type I am glad to say is usually of the " sporting " breed of " boys," and has no relation to decent beings.

With my delayed instalment and my friend's freedom in my hand, I hied me unto the ancient capitalist at Victoria. I made no complaint, for indeed I had no ground. He made no apology, but received my money (I beg pardon, his money) with dignity, saying that he was glad the matter was so speedily arranged, because the aggressive process involved a lot of trouble which he hated. But business was business, and a bargain was a bargain, as he hoped I knew well, and—he hoped the weather would continue fine, being indeed very seasonable for the time of the year. And so we parted, I certainly feeling truly ashamed at having put this good old man to so much unnecessary trouble, my friend to indignity, and myself to so many superfluous blushes.

And as if to compensate me in some measure for what was in truth a heavy day, I found on my arrival home quite a nice order awaiting me. A gentleman of that fine class, the commercial traveller, who had often patronised me before, came in and ordered four pounds worth of pictures, paying as was his wont the money for them upon giving the order, and telling me that I could deliver them any time within the month. By great good fortune I had everything necessary to carry out the order in stock, and as soon as he was gone, I set to work with a glad heart. For I was like a cork, easily depressed, but popping up again serenely as soon as the pressure was removed. However, I could not be allowed even that small interregnum of peace, for at about ten a man came in with some inquiry about my charges for framing. I paid as much attention as I always did to his questions, but unfortunately had to leave him in the shop for a few minutes, while I went into my workshop. When I returned he was gone, and so was my glass-cutting diamond, which was lying upon the baize-covered table on which I cut my glass.

It was a heavy loss to me, for I had got used to its *cut*, and although its price was only 12s. 6d. I never had another that I could use properly, not being at all expert anyhow. I will not deny that this made me feel very unhappy, for when there was so much lying around stealable that would never be missed, I did feel it hard that a fellow should come in and steal my principal tool, for which at the outside he would only be able to realise about three and sixpence in pawn. Still I suppose I ought to be thankful that this was the sole theft I suffered from in all my business career, only somehow the present loss was so great that I was very grieved over it, and moreover I had to send to a local glass-cutter, with whom I was not on any the best terms on account of being a trade rival, for some squares of glass in order to complete my contract in time.

About this month I managed to get a little extra money in a way that seems fantastic, but which came to me as a very welcome addition to my spasmodic earnings. A young gentleman who had been an occasional customer came to me one evening, when I was trying to hammer out an article or story on the counter for want of something more immediately profitable to do, and asked me if I had any objection to model for him. I did not recognise the verb in its present application, and begged him to explain. It then appeared that he was an artist who earned most of his living by illustrating magazines, articles, and stories, and being extremely conscientious, he needed the living model so that his pictures should be vraisembleable as possible. But the professional model was not to be found in East Dulwich, and so in his extremity he thought of me as a man probably eager to earn an honest shilling in whatsoever strange ways.

After a few enquiries I closed with his offer of one and sixpence per hour (always very generously interpreted), and promised to come up to his house as soon as I had closed the shop, or say about 10.30 P.M. I went, and laid the foundation of a friendship that still endures, the artist in question having illustrated several of my books and done so, in my poor opinion, better than any other living artist could have done. But I am getting on too fast.

It must be remembered that as yet I had no experience of " modelling," knew absolutely nothing of what it meant to stand for half an hour in one position, and in parenthesis I may say that I never learned well. But I did my best, and my employer was pleased to say that my intelligent appreciation of what he wanted was much more useful to him than would have been the trained immobility of any professional model. But oh ! how I suffered. I thought I knew what hard work, what endurance was. I got a severe shock. In justice to myself I must ask my readers to remember that I had been up since 6 A.M., and it was now nearly midnight, and that even if I had not been using my thews and sinews all that time I had been up and about. Anyhow I know that after striking an attitude which satisfied my employer and maintaining it for say seven or eight minutes, I felt as if I was in some infernal torture chamber, and though very anxious to *earn* my money and to win approval I had to give in.

But my employer was kindness itself, and though naturally intensely anxious to carry out his ideas, he never took the slightest advantage of my position, or insisted upon any pound of flesh. So far from that, and I cannot tell what it meant to me then, as soon as my time was up I was invited to a good supper, which his charming wife had prepared, and at which I was made to feel a welcome guest, with no thought of that hardly earned eighteen pence in the background. How much this kindly intercourse helped me I have no means of knowing, but the impression it made upon me at the time is no keener than the sense I have now of how kind it was; and I have been an honoured guest in that friend's house for the last ten years.

This seems, in these desultory confessions, a right and fitting place to set forth the fact that in many of my customers I found friends. By which I mean people who think about you, who would take trouble for you, or would make sacrifices to help you, who grieve over your misfortunes and rejoice when you are doing well. And how precious they are. I have always been a great stickler for the proper definitions of words such as Freedom, Love, Friendship, Truth; and I do wish people would not lightly talk of *friends* when they only mean some casual acquaintance who knows little of them and cares less. I can frankly assert that the only pleasant recollections I have of my shop-keeping days, connected with business that is, are associated with the many kindly folks whom I served. Of course my particular business lent itself to closer relations with customers than ordinary shop-keeping, since I had to discuss their desires with them, and give them the benefit of my experience. The one drawback attached to this was that I often spent three or four times as long discussing a trifling order as it was worth; but that was counter-balanced by my sometimes getting a big order with a very small amount of talk.

It did occasionally happen that I, as the Yankees happily and metaphorically put it, struck a snag even in this, and one glaring instance lingers luridly in my memory. A neighbouring tradesman, with whom I was on most friendly terms, very kindly gave me an in-troduction to a well-to-do customer of his at Tulse Hill. My friend was a builder and decorator, and had done a great deal of work for this gentleman, to their mutual satisfaction. So when, one day, his customer asked him about getting some old English frames regilded he recommended me, and did not, in ordinary business fashion, stipulate that he should have a commission upon the transaction. Cheered by my friend's descrip-tion of his customer, I waited upon the latter, and was received in the most jolly fashion as a guest, and not in any patronising spirit, refreshments being pro-

N

duced and some pleasant general talk ensuing. I was then shown the work and asked for an estimate. This I gave after close calculation, and with due consideration of the fact that my customer had probably obtained other estimates before asking for mine.

But to my intense amazement, the gentleman, upon hearing the sum named, immediately said that he could get the work done in the best style for just one quarter of the sum I had named! Now there was nothing for me to do but give him the lie direct had I obeyed my first impulse. But I stifled it, and mildly said that such a price as he had quoted meant gilding with German metal, as the quantity of gold leaf required to cover those frames would cost three times the sum. He, of course, said that he didn't know anything about that, the price given him by a gilder in the Minories was for English gold. I then rose to go, saying that I regretted not being able to go further in the matter. He then said he did not want to disappoint me, and what was the lowest I could do the job for? I replied quietly that I had quoted the lowest possible price for regilding, and one that was less than half what would be demanded by a big West End firm, but that if he cared to have the frames renovated and touched up where necessary I could meet him with an estimate of half the first amount quoted, but explaining fully that this would be in no sense regilding. After a lot of talk he agreed, and I undertook the work.

My kindly gilder, for I could not do the work myself, never having been able to master the delicacy of touch required in this exceedingly technical operation, made every effort, as he always did, to help me to make the best of a bad bargain, cutting his price as I had cut mine. And he did his touching up so well, that when the work was finished I felt that my customer would say that it would have been a waste of money to have had those frames regilded, they looked so well. Now my part of the work so far consisted in getting the six heavy frames to my shop from Tulse Hill, having first removed the pictures from them, and the completion of my task would be to return them, fitting the pictures in again and hanging them; and my share of the profits were almost precisely what a carrier would have charged for the job. But in the meantime, my customer had removed to Clapham Common, and the task of delivering those frames, which required the most careful handling, was thereby vastly increased in difficulty. However, I tackled it successfully by the aid of the gilder, who, wanting his money, agreed to wait at a neighbouring hostelry until I should return with the spoil.

My customer's satisfaction at the way in which the work had been done could not be concealed, and indeed the pictures did look very fine when in position. Then he asked me nonchalantly if I had brought the bill. I handed it to him. He glanced at it and said, " Oh ! you have made a gross mistake. You agreed to do the work for £2 pounds, and this bill is for £5." For a moment I was speechless, and then replied as calmly as I could, " I have made no mistake, sir ; you wanted me to do the work for £2, and I told you it was impossible. I have to pay my gilder £4. 5s., and he is now waiting for the money at the Plough."

" Well," he rejoined casually, " that's nothing to do with me ; you'll get £2 or nothing. You can please yourself."

Now I am anything but a courageous man, but I felt desperate, and although he towered over me like a giant with a very threatening air, I said, quite coolly, " You owe me £5 for work done, and I shall not leave this house until I get it," at which he laughed merrily and retorted, " Ah ! so that's your little game is it ? Very well, stay here until I'm tired of you, then I'll throw you into the road." So I sat down on the nearest chair (I was then in a partly furnished drawing room), and resigned myself to wait. Fortunately, there was a book there, Kipling's " Light that Failed," and I began to read.

Now strange as it my seem, so great is the power of detachment from circumstances over which I have no control that I have always possessed, that I read that book through with the utmost enjoyment, only an occasional cross current of compunction traversing my mind for the weary wait imposed upon my faithful coadjutor. I had finished the book about a quarter of an hour, which means that I had been in the house nearly four hours, when the *gentleman* came in and said, with assumed surprise, " What, you here still ? How much did you say you wanted ? " " £5," I replied quietly. " All right, here you are," he answered, holding out a £5 note to me. I took it, examined it, said " thank you," and walked out of the house.

Tame ending, was it not, to such a dramatic situation, and tamer still the fact that my only sensation was one of satisfaction that I had got the money. I joined my gilder, who was, I regret to say, distinctly the worse for liquor, having had, as he said, no option but to beguile the long afternoon by taking eight special Scotches for the " good of the house." However I explained the situation to him, handed him his money, and made haste home feeling that if ever I had earned fifteen shillings in my life I had done so on this occasion. In conclusion of this episode, I regret to have to add that my friend who had recommended me to this " genial sportsman," as I heard somebody call him, had the grievous misfortune to lose £50 of hardly earned money due to him from the same merry gentleman. I cannot trust myself to comment upon this behaviour which, alas, is all too common among a certain class who habitually live beyond their means and regard the poor tradesman as fair game. If they can only borrow from him as well their delight seems proportionately heightened.

And now I had a sudden gleam of joy, a bit of pleasure so keen that it made me forget for the time all my troubles. I had a story accepted, and it appeared in print. Many of my readers will know what that meant, but I will not believe that any one could have been more delighted than I was. Not that I built up any airy structures of hope, of fame and fortune as an author upon it, but I could not help feeling that it was wonderful how I, without any of the usual educational aids, in competition with the mighty army of able writers ever assaulting harassed editors in London, and under the stress of such stern life-conditions as mine, should have accomplished such a feat. True it was only in a boy's paper, *Young England*, true that the pay was only a guinea, and that I waited six months for it, but the golden glorious fact remained that I saw myself in print.

Perhaps it is strange that I did not then neglect the business which yielded me nothing but debt and disappointment, and throw all my energies into this new channel. A profound distrust of my own abilities, and an idea that this was just a bit of curious good luck may possibly account for my apathy, but whatever it was I know that for a long time I was content to rest upon my laurels in the literary arena and to grub along in the shop. The verb I have used just expresses it; I grubbed and got ever deeper and deeper into the mire, and to the well-meant advice of my friends as to why on earth I did not give up the unequal struggle and go bankrupt before it killed me, I could only render the same answer as before, that bankruptcy spelt workhouse because I should inevitably lose my job.

But one spring morning I received a warning too urgent to be neglected (though I did not heed it then). I was rushing off to the office as usual after four hours of the hardest work and nothing in me since the previous midday meal, except sundry cups of tea, when just in the middle of Green Lane, Dulwich, I felt the world slipping from under me, and with hardly a struggle I was gone for the time. I often thought somewhat resentfully afterwards how much better for me it would have been not to have revived again into a world already over stocked with mediocrities, how easy and pleasant and satisfactory it would have been to have had the ever-gnawing question of how to live settled authoritatively for me. That, however, was not to be, for presently I came to, awoke as it were from a pleasant sleep, and gazed wonderingly around.

There was no one in sight, for it was then a most secluded pathway at that early hour of the day, and I gradually realised my surroundings. I had fallen very pleasantly upon a grassy and weed over-grown patch at the side of the St Olave's playing grounds, so that I was not bemired or disreputable looking. My first thought was of the office, to get there as soon as possible, and make what excuse I could for my late arrival—for I felt that it must be near noon, as I had no means of knowing the time. So I struggled to my feet, only to find that nature had her authoritative say in the matter, for I trembled so that I could not stand erect, and I felt all gone inside. Moreover there was a curious numbness at my finger ends which seemed to me to presage paralysis. Therefore I gave up the office idea and crept back at the easiest pace I could manage to the house of a gentleman in East Dulwich Grove, nearly next door to James Allen's School, who had often patronised me but never, although a local physician of great repute, attended me or any of my family.

He received me with the utmost kindness and bade me lie down after giving me some sal volatile, also forbade me speaking a word until he gave me leave. So I lay on his sofa watching him at work until my over-burdened heart and overstrung nerves had quieted down. Then he cross-examined me as to my mode of life, my health generally, and at the end of my answers, said quietly, " Now, my friend, advice is usually flung away upon such people as you have declared yourself to be, so I will not advise you. But I tell you, from my utmost convictions, that at the rate you are now living, and in the present condition of your vital powers, your time here on earth is limited to one year, or at the outside eighteen months. If, however, you ease off, slow down, don't work like a fiend or race after trains like a madman, you may live the allotted span."

I was about to reply when he interposed, saying

sadly, " I know you'll tell me it's a counsel of perfection. It's one of the tragedies of our profession
that we continually have to give counsel which the
patient cannot follow. But we cannot help that.
Now, I'll listen to what you have got to say." And
he did. I detailed to him as to a father confessor,
the uttermost particulars of my business, my debts,
and the conditions under which I held my clerkship.
He listened most sympathetically, most kindly, and
then threw up his hands with a gesture as of one
compelled to dismiss the case from his mind.

# CHAPTER XIV

## RELIEF AT LAST

"HEART failure; mustn't hurry or you'll die; must eat more, whether you've any appetite, or means to get it or not; must rest and take things quietly," and so on, and so on. Bitterly I smiled to myself as I slowly crept home. But so curiously is the average man constituted that I did not feel as if I was actually under sentence of death. I rather clung to the belief that Doctor Stericker might be mistaken, and anyhow that many things might happen in eighteen months. Though really that was not what kept me going. I have no claim to perseverance, pertinacity, courage or, least of all, optimism, but like the involved orator I couldn't see a place to leave off. No opening presented itself to me to step out of and lay the almost intolerable burden down, although I know full well that but for those helpless ones dependent upon me I should certainly have made or found a way long before.

Here is the only explanation I can give of my persistence in a hopeless cause, to assign any other would be rank hypocrisy, as it would be to claim any special virtues of endurance or bravery in the face of overwhelming odds. And I have often thought that in many of us who get credit for " sticking to it " when all hope seems dead, there may be something of what Kipling quotes as the pertinacity of materials : we hold on because it has become a habit so to do. But even I could not help seeing that the crash could now not be very long delayed, especially as I dared no longer dash at my work when it came in with a rush. I have also to recall very gratefully that my chief at the office, who took a kindly interest in my struggles, and had advised me to file my petition in bankruptcy, now hinted to me very clearly that in the event of my doing so, no notice would be taken by those " up above." This cheered me immensely, for I knew he would not have told me this if he had not found good grounds for doing so. And so I went on in my quieter course awaiting the catastrophe, and absolutely uncertain as to how or when it would come.

Just about this time, I was delighted by the acceptance of an article I had written, by the editor of *Chambers's Journal*, a magazine which I had known and admired all my life, although I think it was called *Chambers's Miscellany*, " When that I was a little tiny boy," I had also imagined that the publication of a story or an article by anybody in those familiar double-column pages conferred a sort of brevet rank upon the writer of which no one could rob him ; and in addition to all this the cheque which I received with (to me) amazing promptitude, was three times as much as I had previously received for an article of nearly the same length. So that altogether I felt uplifted and heartened, although the idea of literature as a profession still never occurred to me, especially as I was rapidly nearing forty, and feeling very often double that.

I fully believed that at forty a man's career was irrevocably fixed ; if he had done nothing worthy of note before, he would certainly never do anything after, and all the stirring adventure of my early days had been completely overlaid by the dull drab round of my clerkly duties through so many years, to say nothing of the other jejune, undramatic, commonplace matters of which I have been writing in these pages. Only, and this I would like to lay stress upon, there was a glow of strange delight in my heart, to find that when I took my pen in hand and sat down to write, all that early life on many seas stood out bold and clear upon the background of my mind, and I lived its incidents over and over again.

Little did any of my infrequent customers think when they came into the shop and saw me writing as if for dear life, as I leaned over the counter, that I was lost in the resuscitated life of a quarter of a century before. And strange to say, at least to me, as soon as I laid down the pen all the vivid reality vanished, and I was as eager to get an order for a five-shilling frame, or to sell a couple of little pictures that I had framed on speculation, as if I had never done anything else all my life. Occasionally, however, my eagerness departed, as when one day a lady came in and purchased all the framed Mildmay texts I had in the place, telling me that she was going to present them to a church bazaar. Of course I cut the price to the bone, as we say, for I thought I must not miss so good a chance of getting rid of stock that had been on hand for a long time; so I charged her just about half what the things cost me in materials. Her order came to thirty shillings, and she said when about to pay me, " Of course you'll give me twenty-five per cent. discount, I always get that for bazaar goods ! "

Even £1. 2s. 6d. would have been heartily welcome, but I rejoice to recollect that I told that wicked old harpy exactly what I thought of her, and her methods, and the system generally. This is not the place nor the time for a dissertation upon the charity of those who grind the face of the poor tradesman to supply the goods which they so ostentatiously present to the local bazaar, but I do not know that anything has aroused fiercer resentment in my heart than the behaviour of these liars, hypocrites, and thieves. Strong words, I agree, but not any stronger than the truth which is, as we know, mighty and will prevail.

Nearer and nearer drew the day of my deliverance,

though of the manner in which that liberation was to be effected or of the time when it would come, I had not the remotest idea.   I have omitted to say that when I took this shop I agreed with the gas company to supply me with three large incandescent gas lamps on hire.   They gave a splendid light, and were called the Vertmarsche patent, I remember.   I was very proud of them, although they were only mine by courtesy, as I had not paid more than three quarterly instalments off their heavy cost.   But they certainly did give a tone to the appearance of the shop, and although they undoubtedly made a heavy increase in my gas bills, I had learned that economy in light in any shop was fatal to business.

However I was often congratulated upon the splendour of my lights, for the system was then new, and I was the only tradesman in the lane who had them.   They were especially admired by the tenant of my old shop nearly opposite, who had for some time been endeavouring to carry on a little drapery business there.   He used to come over and swap troubles with me, telling me things which made me realise that I was by no means the only sufferer in this war of ours.   At last, one evening, he became exceedingly confidential, telling me that his affairs had come to a crisis, and that he was about to file his petition in bankruptcy.   But, he said, his furniture was of a very good and expensive kind, and he felt it would be too bad to have it seized and sold for such a trifle as it would surely fetch at a knockout auction. Would I then let him my first-floor front room, which I had never occupied, as a store house for the best of his furniture until the clouds had rolled away ? and if so, what would I charge per week. He could pay three shillings and sixpence.

At first I hesitated, for I realised the precariousness of my own position, but my visitor, mistaking my hesitation for a desire to get more money out of him, said, " I'd pay you more if I could, but I swear I have hardly a penny in the world. Do help me if you can ; you may be glad of a similar lift yourself some day." Of course I hastened to assure him that nothing could well have been farther from my thoughts than the idea of exploiting his misery. Three shillings and sixpence a week would pay me well, and indeed was the sum I had been vainly asking for that room for a long time.

He thanked me effusively and departed. After closing hours, he managed to get his effects transferred to my front room, and when I saw the kind of stuff he had, I could not wonder at his anxiety lest it should fall into the hands of those harpies, who batten upon the hardships of people who have their homes broken up. A terrible tragedy indeed, when the savings of an industrious lifetime invested in furniture are knocked down for, in many cases, less shillings than they cost pounds originally, and are then immediately resold to the inner gang for an enhanced price, to appear in a few days' time in some local furnishing warehouse at almost as high a price as their original figure.

The next day, my poor little guest came the expected cropper. His shop was closed, and he disappeared with his wife and family. I felt a wistful curiosity to know how he was faring, and yet a curious diffidence lest I should learn too much for my peace of mind. And so he passed out of my thoughts, and indeed I even forgot that so large a portion of his belongings was under my roof. Truly I had quite sufficient of my own pressing personal affairs to occupy all my attention to the exclusion of any one else's troubles for the time, and that probably made me more callous than I should have been. I know that when some chance acquaintance would come in, and after a very lengthy preamble, try to borrow a few shillings, I used to wax eloquent. Yet I suppose I ought to have been quite grateful for the opportunity of giving utterance to my sorrows without being suspected of ulterior motives. But I regret to say that I got a very bad idea of my fellow-men generally about this time. So many of them known to me looked so jolly, existed so easily, dressed well, smoked good cigars, and yet when they got me by myself invariably sang a song of misery, of a hollow mask concealing a broken heart, which the temporary loan of a pound or two would mend. And when the pound or two was not forthcoming a shilling or even sixpence would be so welcome.

One quality they certainly had, that of perseverance. Yes, after the most vehement exposition of the impossibility of ever borrowing anything from me, of all people in the world, they would reappear shortly on the same errand, until I shrewdly suspected, and told them as much, that they were only doing it for practice.

The climax for which I had been so long and so ignorantly waiting came in dramatic fashion. Not, of course, as I had expected it to come, for to tell the plain simple truth I had for a long time thought that it would arrive by my falling dead in the street, and I exercised my imagination continually on the possible scenes afterwards. There was nothing much to wonder at in this for I almost always felt at this time as if I was, as the Spaniards say, *Gastados*, used up, had nothing at all left inside. But on this eventful evening I was working away as usual, " fitting up," in trade terms, at my glass cutting bench, when, without the slightest warning, the whole ceiling of the shop fell down, from wall to wall it tore away in one great mass of rotten plaster, smashing everything in its fall and filling the shop with dust and ruin. An earthquake could not have been more comprehensive as regards the internal fittings of the shop. My blessings upon the loafing scoundrels who slapped that rubbish up against the laths above, entirely careless of what happened as long as it stuck there till they got their money. They did me better service

o

than they ever dreamed of. A big chunk of plaster having hit me on the head I was for a moment dazed and partly suffocated by the dust as well, but I saw my broken lamps flaring up towards the network of tindery laths above, and insinctively I dropped on my hands and knees to grope my way to the gas meter. I got rather badly cut, but I found the meter and turned off the gas, just in time to save the house from catching fire.

I can hear some cynic say, "Silly ass, why didn't he let it catch fire and burn down, he could have made a bit out of it then." Perhaps so, but I was not prepared to make a bit, and I had trained myself in habits of honesty (now don't laugh, for many people do, and I am no great exception) so that my first and only thought at that juncture was to prevent the greater calamity of fire. Groping my way back along the counter, the dust having somewhat subsided I saw my wife, white and trembling, at the door of the shop parlour. On a sudden impulse I laughed loudly. In that instant I saw that the long looked for deliverance had come at last. But she said, "Oh, what's the matter? Are you all right? meaning was I sane. I answered cheerily, "No doubt about that. I'm all right, and for good or evil I've done with this business. This means a full stop. I can't go on, however much I might want to."

Then I became aware that the outside of the shop was crowded with people who had heard the crash,

and with the intense curiosity of a London crowd had
accumulated with the idea of seeing what was " up."
This sight caused my mirth to subside, for like most
Englishmen I hate a crowd, hate to be pried upon,
especially at a time like that. We like to fight our
troubles alone, or at most with one or two chosen
chums. On the platform it is different, the more
facing you then the better, but afterwards, half a
dozen will make you feel awkward. So I went to
the door, and said appealingly, " What do you want ? "
There was no reply, so with a sigh I went on. " The
ceiling of my shop has fallen down and ruined my
stock. That's all. There's plenty of trouble, but
it's mine, and you people can only add to it by crowd-
ing round here." With this I seized my " long arm,"
a pole with a hook to it, and marching out pulled the
shutters down. I daresay a lot of them stood for a
long time staring at the shutters, a practice of London
crowds that is in curious variance to their usual alert-
ness, but I do not know, for I did not look out again
that night.

Having bolted up as securely as if I feared a raid
I came back to the parlour, where my wife met me,
still with that doubting look in her eyes, and said,
" Whatever will you do ? " " *Do*," I replied, " I
shall do the only thing that is now possible, I shall
go up to Bankruptcy Buildings in the morning and
file my petition." " How do you do that ? " she
queried. " I don't know anything about it, but I

can learn, and shall learn I doubt not pretty quick,"
I answered. "And in any case it doesn't matter
much now, for I am absolutely certain that this is
what I have been unconsciously waiting for so long."
As the matter was not yet quite plain to her I went on
to point out the absolutely ruinous condition of the
house with respect to the other ceilings, which did
not, however, make the place uninhabitable. The
shop was quite another matter. For in the first
place the bulk of my stock of pictures was smashed,
in the next my three costly lamps would require at
least £5 spent upon them to put them in working order again, while I could not possibly open
the shop again for business in that forlorn and
dilapidated condition.

Now the landlord had simply scoffed at the idea
of doing anything to the premises in the way of
repairs, telling me, with some indignation, what was
indeed true, that the house had just been practically
rebuilt, although taking no notice of my demur that
the work had been so badly done that it had long ago
required doing all over again. In addition to all
these things I was very near the end of a second
quarter in which I had paid no rent, and I should
have been diffident, to put it delicately, in any case
of approaching the landlord upon the subject of repairs
unless I could do so with £20 in my hand.

To say that I had no money wherewith to get
these repairs done would be too bold a platitude, for

I never had any money that I could call my own, I never spent a penny upon the imperative needs of my family or myself, without a sense of guilt, of dishonesty, because I knew that it rightly belonged to someone else. But perhaps I should not have accepted the fiat of that collapsed ceiling so readily, had I not, metaphorically speaking, been in a state of physical decay, and inviting a *coup de grâce*. At anyrate I was perfectly satisfied in my own mind that it was a direct interposition of the awful power of Providence in my little ephemeral affairs, and after a few mouthfuls of bread and cheese I went to bed with a lighter heart than I had borne for many a day.

I arose in the morning at daylight, refreshed by my good rest, which in itself was most unusual, but to me is a proof how largely fatigue is induced by worry. My first thought was the ruin below, and as soon as I had drunk my tea, I faced it. Pushing the shutters up and letting the light stream in, I surveyed the scene and saw that it was far more ghastly than I had realised last night. In fact it quite fascinated me, and I stood staring at it for about ten minutes, softly whistling the while, until I suddenly came to myself with a jerk, and commenced to clear up a bit. But it was a painful business because of its obvious hopelessness. Still something had to be done in order to get in and out, and besides I had got so used to work that employment, whether remunerative or not, was an absolute necessity.

Another thing which made this occupation so painful to me was the handling of the broken children of my labours, my picture frames. Every one of them had been a source of pride to me as I finished it, and stood it up to contemplate it ; and to see them all mutilated, spoiled, and scattered was to me a most depressing sight. Still, by sheer force of habit, I worked on, and succeeded in getting a sufficient clearance made for present purposes by the time I had to prepare for the office. Not that I intended to do any office work that day, for quite different plans were in my mind.

I reached the office at the usual time, and, without uncovering my table, sought my kindly chief and told him that I was at last compelled to take his often reiterated advice and go to Carey Street (the Bankruptcy Court). Hurriedly I explained the circumstances to him, finding that he was entirely in favour of my action. Then I made out the usual application for a day's leave (to be deducted from my summer vacation), handed it in, and left.

With ample time to spare, I strolled up to the huge pile of buildings at the back of the Law Courts, which I in common with many happier Londoners had never known the use of until then. Indeed they had not long been finished and the approach to them, across what some of the newspapers ironically called at that time Strand Common, was quite appropriately depressing. It had that effect upon me at anyrate, added to all that horror of the unknown which is so natural to imaginative people and withal so unjustifiable in nine cases out of ten. Being full early I sat down on one of the benches which even then were provided by some thoughtful souls for the use of weary jetsam from the roaring tide of the Strand or Fleet Street, and endeavoured to concentrate my thoughts upon the approaching ordeal. It was a hopeless failure, as any attempts at meditation have always been with me. My thoughts will only flow under the stimulus of speech or pen action, in silence and alone they are uncontrollable, and range fruitlessly over the whole field of my experience.

But, behold, to me came sudden and grateful relief in the person of an old patron of mine who held some snug billet as an official reporter at the Law Courts facing us. Having an hour to spare, he had come there to smoke a contemplative pipe and enjoy the unwonted rest from recording in wiggly hieroglyphics the mass of banalities, lies, and legalities which it was his business to perpetuate in print. He was an enthusiast in photography — indeed, it was his only hobby—and at the very slightest sign that I was attending to what he said, he launched forth into a flood of talk about lenses and exposures, and focussing and developing, about all of which I knew rather less than I did of cuneiform inscriptions. But he was so pleased, and my face expressed so much interest (which I swear I could not feel), that he babbled on for the hour he had to spare.

Then suddenly he said, "But what are you doing here?" I replied casually as if it was an ordinary occurrence with me, "Oh, I'm waiting to file my petition in Bankruptcy as soon as it's eleven o'clock." "Indeed," he answered, "well, you needn't be in a hurry, you won't find anybody in there that is. Good morning," and he left me.

True my histrionic qualities are few, but I know that I did try and impart a pathetic break to my voice when I spoke of my errand, to infuse it with a pathos which I did not feel, for I had no idea of what was before me. I know also that he did not take the slightest notice of my tone, and treated it as one of the commonest of human experiences, one not deserving of even a passing thought. I know too that this vulgar indifference of his hurt me more than any words of whatever kind could have done. By it I knew that I was now enrolled among the ranks of the great army who live by their wits, who make a business of living upon other people, who are as much the parasites of society as the bookmaker or the bucket-shopkeeper, although not nearly so prosperous. No one would give me any credit, I knew, for the almost superhuman struggles I had made to pay my way, and to justify my right to live and maintain my wife and family. I, who had literally starved myself and worked myself into collapse in order to practice all the week what I preached on Sundays in the open air, was now to be classed with those whom I had so often denounced.

Perhaps it served me right for denouncing anybody. But it is hard when one feels deeply to refrain from speech. Yet I suppose it would be safe to say that we never know what we might become if we fell victims to the *folie des grandeurs*, combined with that far more common complaint, the accursed thirst for gold, no matter whose.

## CHAPTER XV

## LEGAL EXPERIENCES

STANDING, as I am now (as far as my story is concerned), on the threshold of the Bankruptcy Court, I wish to disavow the idea of having any quarrel with individuals, or, of any personal bias. One of the main objects I have had before me in writing this book has been to record simply and without hyperbole my own experiences in connection with this great national Institution. If, in the course of my remarks, I say anything which is not strictly warranted by the facts, I declare that it is not intentional. I only say that which personal observation and experience leads me to believe is strictly true. Also, be it noted, I write from the point of the view of the amateur—I have not had the benefit in one sense of an association with any of those able financiers who have been bankrupt several times, and then have retired to enjoy in a peaceful retirement the fruits of their labours.

I declare that when I pushed open the swing doors of the vast hall I felt just as a boy does upon entering a school for the first time. So utterly ignorant, so helpless, so willing to learn. I advanced a few paces and met a cheery soul in uniform, who said heartily, " Wotyer lookin' fur, Govnor ? " Now, as the Americans say, wouldn't that get you busy ? I looked at him and to him, I make no doubt, like a perfect fool. He looked at me keenly and enquiringly, until I had to say, " Well, the fact is—I am unfamiliar with these places, but I have had misfortunes and I wish to file my petition in Bankruptcy." You will observe from its frequent repetition how proud I was of having got what I considered one legal phrase at least pat and complete. He replied with the utmost nonchalance, " Right O, second door on the left, and ask at the desk. They'll put you up to it."

I followed his instructions, feeling that I was getting on, and entered the room he indicated. There were several men, I dare not say clerks for they had not any of the characteristics of that much derided tribe, and I doubt whether even Mr H. G. Wells would have satirised them in his usual curious fashion concerning clerks, but all were engaged, nay engrossed with some work, until I came to the last, and he was reading the *Daily Chronicle*. As I was only one of his employers, I acted as usual, that is, I humbly waited before him until he had finished the article he was reading, when he languidly lifted his eyes to me and said with an air, not exactly of contempt, but of the most utter and complete detachment, " Well ! what is your business ? "

Still with bated breath and lowly demeanour, I

replied, " I wish to file my petition in Bankruptcy."
" All right," he answered as he folded his paper,
" that'll be £10 — £5 for the stamp and £5
security for costs." I caught my breath and said,
" But I've got no money at all; I can't pay
anybody, that is why I came here." To which he
rejoined casually, " Who's your solicitor ? " This,
I am afraid, rather disturbed me, for how I, who had
avowed myself penniless, could afford to pay a solicitor
(the very word savoured of affluence to me) I could not
conceive, and I did really regard his question as an in-
solent one. It was not, of course. It was perfectly
business like and proper from his point of view,
which from mine was as wide as the poles asunder.
But still, realising my position, I told him civilly that
I had no money to employ a solicitor, that so far from
having £10, my stock of ready cash was under
five shillings, that if I had £10 I should certainly
not be there, but handing that £10 out to some of
those who were entitled to it.

Much more I said to the same non-effect, for he
listened with an expression of infinite weariness, and
when I had finished he said abruptly, " How much do
you owe ? " I answered, about £300. " Very well,
then," he replied, " if you had £10 wouldn't it be
much better to come to us with it and empower us
to treat with your creditors than to fritter that crumb
away paying two or three and annoying all the rest ?
But, after all, that's not the point ; it's none of my duty

to stand here telling you what you ought to do. You get £10 and come here with it, and I'll give you your papers and set you going. Good morning."

Thus he ceased and busied himself with a heap of papers, leaving me standing aghast at the idea that a man who had no money to pay his debts should have to pay £10 for the privilege of saying so in public, that any money he might have should not be devoted to paying his debts, but to making legal excuses why he should not do so. However, this particular official had obviously had quite sufficient of such a fool as I was, and it was of no use wasting time there, so I quietly slunk away in worse plight than ever, to my way of thinking. For I could not possibly bring my mind to bear upon the inherent dishonesty of the situation.

As thus—declaring myself a bankrupt, all my belongings of whatever kind as well as my future earnings, until my debts were satisfied, became automatically the property of the official receiver to hold in trust for my creditors. Therefore to sell it, or any portion of it for any purpose, was a felony. Yet having no money how was I to raise these fees? I could not borrow, for if I revealed my position, no sane person would lend, and I could not possess any security. If anybody gave me money for the purpose of paying those fees, it would be a fraud upon my creditors to put the money to that purpose. Whichever way I looked I could see no way out but by falsehood and fraud, and I was only at the beginning of my experience.

In this extremity I went to a man of great experience in business, but with a high reputation for probity as far as meeting all his liabilities went. He was also credited with very sharp practice despite his high moral and religious standing. Consequently, I do not suppose I could have consulted any one better qualified to give me advice. He fully agreed with me that nothing was more eminently calculated to destroy the moral sense than going through the Bankruptcy Court, of your own initiative—if your creditors made you a bankrupt it was another matter. In a case like mine it was obvious that a man had to pay a considerable sum down for the privilege of swearing that he had no money at all, which money could not legally be his. Yet, since the law itself created this dishonest state of affairs, I was clearly absolved from the charge of dishonesty if I raised and paid this money, providing those from whom I obtained it were not defrauded by being made the victims of false representations on my part.

He finished his advice by lending me £2 towards the amount required, and I went on my sorrowful way homewards. When I reached home I found a fresh batch of dunning letters and two judgment summonses waiting for me, but I paid no heed to them, I had more engrossing business to attend to. I spent a long time explaining the position to my wife and endeavouring to furbish up some of the stock in the event of my being driven to raise money on it, and then went on the doleful business of trying to borrow £8 without any reasonable prospect of being able to repay it. That was indeed a pilgrimage of pain. But I must not say that; although the fruit of a long half day's search was only £1, I met with very much sympathy and many kind cheering words, also much commendation for having taken the step I had at last.

I went back to the office in the morning, after a sleepless night, feeling as unfit for my clerical duties as I could well be, as may be imagined. My sympathetic chief was of course anxious to know how I had fared, and listened with the greatest attention to my story. Then he suggested that I had better take at least a couple of days off, as I could not possibly do my work under such mental conditions, and leave no means untried to raise that money, even if I had to sell such of the stock as I could make saleable at any price it would fetch. And he wound up by lending me a sovereign, to be repaid when I could.

So I got through the day somehow, though I am afraid I sorely exasperated other care-free individuals, who had to work with me and could not realise the condition of my mind. At last five o'clock came, and I hurried home. My wife met me midway of the shop with a beaming face, and held out her hand with eight sovereigns in it. I staggered back as if I had received a blow, and gasped, "Wh-a-at, where, how did you get it?" "Pawned the piano," she replied promptly, a statement which filled me with amazement, for, although I was only too familiar with the side entrance to establishments flaunting the three golden balls, she, to the best of my knowledge and belief, had never been in such a place in her life. I had always taken that unpleasant necessity upon myself.

But there was the money, the price of deliverance, and now I must explain the circumstances. The piano was an exceedingly good one which I had bought on the hire system long ago at the second-hand price of £40. I had presented it to her on some anniversary and thenceforward never thought of it as mine, never regarded it as a possible means of raising money for my needs. And here it had been the saving of a very bad situation, for although my experience was still green I dimly understood that the hour of deliverance was at hand. The side-issue of the terribly low figure for which that beautiful instrument was pledged —which if not repaid within a year would mean its loss —did touch me rather sharply, but I could not stop to think of that, nor could I be ungrateful enough to suggest to my wife that she might have done better, remembering her experience. Also I felt that in a year, who knew, I might happen on something which would enable me to redeem the piano.

So I had the price, and secure in that knowledge I went to bed and slept very soundly, no thought of the proceedings after the preliminary payment occasioning me the slightest uneasiness. And it was with a light heart that I rose early in the morning to complete the clearing up of my wrecked ship, to put, in fact, my house in order against what I dimly foresaw would be the next step, the visit of the official assessor whose duty it would be to estimate the whole of my possessions, with the exceptions of tools and an irreducible minimum of clothing and bedding, not bedsteads. By eleven o'clock I had made the poor place look quite respectable and hurried off, leaving, as a last message, instructions to my wife to dispose of our fowls for what they would fetch. We had bred them ourselves, and they had been a source of great pleasure to us and profit to the children, for they responded liberally in the matter of eggs. There were twenty-five of them altogether, beautiful birds of no particular breed, and all pets. I may as well finish off this particular transaction by saying that during the day they were sold *en bloc* for eighteen shillings, although any one of them would have cost three shillings dead had I been a buyer.

Away I went in high spirits to Carey Street, but before I got there, I felt the malign influence of the place upon me, and when I entered those fateful doors, I was subdued enough. No need for me to enquire the way now, I went straight to the desk of the official whom I had encountered before. He looked at me with the same air of nonchalant aloofness, as of a

P

being from another sphere beyond all such hopes and fears and sorrows as I might have. Producing the money, I said submissively, " I have brought the fees you told me were necessary." " Ah, I think I remember something about it," he replied. " Wanted to file your own petition, didn't you ? " Of course I retold my story, or as much of it as he would listen to, until he interrupted me with, " Who's your solicitor ? " Again I assured him that I had no money wherewith to employ a solicitor, and, moreover, I had been assured that the business was so simple that any man of ordinary intelligence could manage it himself.

He gave me a pitying glance, and then grunted, " Oh, all right. Take these forms and fill them up. Anything you don't understand, I'll try to explain to you." So saying he handed me a most formidable sheaf of printed documents, wherein I read in the usual involved official verbiage all sorts of instructions as to my procedure. I had been fairly well accustomed to official forms, but my heart sank at the sight of these, for it seemed an utter impossibility that I should ever make head or tail of them.

However I attacked them boldly, and when I came to a snag I just left it and went on to the next. By the end of an hour, I had done something to all the forms, but it was very little, and I took them back to the man at the desk with a modest request that he would explain some of the difficulties to me. As he glanced over the sheets a deep frown gathered over his brow, and he presently growled. " Look here, why the devil don't you get a solicitor ?  You'll never do this yourself, and I can't be bothered showing you. I've got my work to do."   (In my innocence I had imagined that what I was asking him to do was his work.) I patiently explained to him my position once more, for though naturally prone to resent injustice and high-handed officialdom, my spirit was sadly broken and lent itself to being bullied, up to a certain point.

So he did some more explaining, but with very bad grace, and with a manner exactly like that of a coarse-minded usher with a very dull and frightened small boy. I paid all the attention I could, took the forms away, and had another hour at them.  Then I came to an absolute deadlock, and though I very much disliked going to him again, I was compelled to do so.  He took the documents from me in grim silence, glanced at them, and then said with much emphasis, " Oh ! this'll never do. Messenger ! "  The messenger appearing, my mentor queried of him, " Is old hard-hat about ? "   " I think so," replied the messenger. "Well, go and tell him I want him," and the messenger departed.

Pending his return I waited, still like the school-boy at the master's desk, wondering mightily who " old hard-hat " might be, and what he could have to do with me, or I with him.  As he was rather long in coming, I grew mildly impatient, and ventured to ask who had been sent for. The man behind the desk replied sharply, "You've got to be identified, and you can't possibly do that yourself." "Well," I answered, "how in the name of common sense can a man whom I have never seen or heard of identify me?"

"Oh," he grunted, "you've got nothing to do with that. It's just a legal form, that's all." I might have said some more, but just then the person we were waiting for arrived. A tall slender figure in brown, with an auburn wig and no teeth. He had a placid yet decided way with him, and reminded me, oddly enough, of Charles Lamb, from what I had read of that gentle soul, and such portraits as I had seen of him.

Coming direct to my mentor, the new comer said, "You sent for me, I believe, Mr Blank." "Yes," replied the clerk, "take this man away, and see if you can get him out of the muddle he is in with those documents." Mr Hardhat, for so I must call my new acquaintance, turned to me and murmured, "Will you come over to this table with me?" I went, but on arriving there, I said, "Look here, before we go any further, are you a solicitor sent for to help me?" He replied, to the best of my recollection, that he was, but not in regular business; in short I gathered, I do not know how, that he had either never passed his examination, or that he had for some reason not been able to carry on a regular business, and that he now attended that building regularly in the hope of picking up such chance jobs as mine promised to be.

Upon finding this out, I immediately made it plain to him that I was utterly unable to incur a solicitor's bill, that I had been told by people in authority that there was nothing in Bankruptcy procedure to prevent an unhappy debtor from doing his own business; and although I had not in the least realised what an unpleasant business it was, I was bound to go through with it. He heard me out with great patience, and then said mildly, "Yes, I know that theoretically it is possible for a debtor to do his own business here, but practically it is not possible. As to paying me for the assistance I can give you, please don't let that trouble you at all. I am quite willing to do my best for you, and let the question of payment (it will be a mere trifle in any case) stand over until you come upon happier times. If you never pay me it will not ruin me, and I might as well be helping you as doing nothing. Please let us get to work, and say no more about it."

I really cannot say how deeply touched I was by this man's gentle kindness, and the more because of its contrast with my treatment by the well-paid official, and I made a mental vow that if ever I were able to repay him, I would be as lavish in doing so as my circumstances would permit. Then I told him that I could not be so brutally independent as to throw his kindness back at him, and I would accept his help with gratitude. He nodded gravely, took the papers from me, drew his fountain pen from his pocket, and sat down to work.

Now for anything I know it may be necessary to make the formulæ of bankruptcy proceedings as difficult, technical, and prolix as possible, not being an expert I dare not offer an opinion, but I do know that this expert who had now come to my assistance, although working with great skill and rapidity, took several hours to prepare the documents demanded, and then much of what was put down was fiction, had to be, since I had kept no books, and even though my memory was phenomenally good, it was far from equal to the demands now made upon it. But at last the dread business was complete, we took those forms to another official who merely glanced through them, secured them together with green cord, and handed us a piece of parchment (I believe) which we had to write certain matters upon, and then take to another part of the building to be stamped.

Up till now I had only paid £5, but now I was to disburse another £5 for the privilege of becoming a bankrupt, the first £5 having been as security for costs. So we handed the mystic document we bore to a man who looked like a superior workman, who took it from us, and held out his hand for my £5. When I had paid him, he took a stamp from a drawer, and after pumice-stoning the parchment in a certain place, and doing something else to the back of the stamp, carried the latter over to where a glue-pot stood simmering on a gas ring.   Here he anointed the stamp, placed it on the document, put the latter in a press, and then obliterated the stamp in two or three other ways.   I never saw so much work upon a stamp before.   But then, to be sure, it was a stamp representing £5 sterling.

This operation was almost the last for the day, which was now wearing to a close.   My good friend, Mr Hardhat, merely took the last document to another part of the building while I waited for him.   When he returned he told me that my preliminary examination was fixed for the second day afterwards at eleven in the morning, and that until then nothing further could be done.   But he also assured me that I was now *ipso facto* bankrupt, and that I was on no account to pay anybody anything on account of debt, for that would be a misdemeanour.   If any of my creditors took action, with the exception of the landlord, who might distrain for his overdue rent, I had only to show them a certain slip of paper I possessed, and that would, in sea-metaphor, choke their luffs.

I thanked him, and made for home, determined to devote the next day to some good hard work at the bench, framing up such pictures and texts as I had in stock, so as to use up the remainder of my moulding, backboard, glass, etc.   And then I should perhaps be able to make a forced sale, and raise some ready money. With these thoughts in my mind, I turned the corner of Ashbourne Grove into Lordship Lane, and not looking where I was going, I ran into a man whom I at once recognised as the lessee of my former shop and my present first floor front room. We greeted one another heartily, and he said, " Let's see, I owe you a week's rent, here it is," and he placed three and sixpence in my hand. He went on, " I shan't want you to store that furniture for more than a week or two longer, for I am very nearly through my difficulties, and I am thinking of taking a nice little business in Dalston." As soon as he had said this, I remarked gravely, " I don't want to frighten you, but if you'll take my advice you'll shift those sticks out of where they are now with the least possible delay. I told you when you put them there that I was in Queer Street, and to-day I have been adjudicated bankrupt. Now, you know what that means."

He stared at me wildly for a moment, as if he had seen a ghost, and then cried, " Merciful heavens, I must hurry up." Off he rushed down the lane, leaving me laughing to think of my experience of the lame leading the blind. But I was very glad of his three and six all the same, and not having eaten all day save for a crust of bread and cheese at noon, I determined that something hot for supper should be forthcoming. Procuring the materials for this meal took me some little time, and when I arrived at the shop, my poor little tenant drew up at the door with a coal-trolly, which he had hired somewhere on the spur of the moment. I at once opened the side door for him and it was really a sight to see how he toiled to get his household goods out, especially in contrast with the calm deliberateness of the coal-heaver.

When it was all on the trolly, he gave a great sigh of relief, and came into the shop mopping his streaming head. "Well, old chap," he gasped, "that's as narrow a squeak as I want; and I can't blame anybody but myself, for I ought to have let you know where to find me. However, it's all right now, and I only hope you'll get through your trouble as I've done. Good-bye." And he went out of my life.

I worked very hard the next day for two reasons, first, I did want to get as much stuff ready for sale as possible, my sense of absolute honesty having already become considerably blunted by contact with that temple of fraud in Carey Street; and secondly, because I did not want to brood over the terrible possibility of my landlord coming in by deputy and seizing all my poor belongings—for in my simplicity I still looked upon them as mine, totally oblivious of the fact that, in the eyes of the law, I now possessed absolutely nothing except necessary clothing and bedding, tools and cooking utensils. Now and then the thought would obtrude itself that after all these years of toil and stress, I had brought, vulgarly speaking, my pigs to a pretty fine market, but my sense of relief from the misery I had so long endured outweighed any other consideration, and I was not at all melancholy.

My day's work was a fruitful one, for I managed to knock up quite a number of little frames for which, if low in price, I was fairly sure of a ready sale for that reason. And I also put the last touches on my tidying up, as well as getting ready such small goods as I knew I should be allowed to retain. I also secured a place of refuge—a house to move into—from a local house agent, secured it too without the slightest concealment from him of all my circumstances. But then he was a good fellow, and never backward in doing a good turn if he could. Thus at the end of the day I felt ready for the crisis of to-morrow. Hitherto there had only been verbiage writing and payment of fees; to-morrow, Mr Hardhat informed me, would see definite action being taken. But of that I will write in the next chapter.

# CHAPTER XVI

## THROUGH TO FREEDOM

I SUPPOSE that there are few things more demoralising to an assimilative mind than the association with places of a demoralising tendency. Which I do not intend as a profound remark, but as the fruit of actual experience. At any rate I know that when I first entered the Bankruptcy Court, I felt a profound pity for the listless, hopeless, slouching-looking figures I saw haunting its purlieus. But when I went up this morning, for my preliminary examination, I felt as listless, hopeless, and slouching as any of them— I had enlisted in the great army of the insolvent, and no matter how void of offence my conscience might be, in that I had not wilfully or in extravagance defrauded any man, the taint of debt, the virus of unutterable meanness which makes the Chinese commit suicide, bowed my head, rounded my shoulders, and robbed me of my self-respect.

I only had to wait about two hours this morning before my turn came on. When it did, and I was summoned to stand before an inquisitor, I received a sudden shock. For, behold, the dread Rhadamanthus to whom I must unveil my most secret sorrows and troubles was a young man whom I had often seen coming up Victoria Street with a similar individual, and had loathed from the depths of my soul. His garb was immaculate as regards the latest fashion, his collar as high as human endurance would permit, his trousers creased in exactly the right line, turned up to exactly the proper height; he slouched at exactly the angle prescribed by his class (or the class to which he wished to appear to belong), and, crowning iniquity, he wore a monocle in his left eye. Altogether a " Johnny " of the Johnniest. And he was my inquisitor !

He took several huge sheets of paper (printed forms of course), and began what I saw was a stereotyped set of questions with a bored air and yet an unpersonal way with him, almost as if he were addressing a penny-in-the-slot machine, which was rather helpful. I was a long time before him, and I answered his questions to the best of my ability, but often I fear with a desire to get the examination over rather than with any keen attention to accuracy. It was a curious business altogether, perfunctory in the extreme, and I had then no idea what my answers would be used for. I learned later.

When released I sought my faithful friend, who advised me to get home with all speed, for that an official appraiser would call upon me that afternoon, and it would be well that I should meet him. So I returned with haste, reaching home a long time before the individual indicated. I must say I awaited him with considerable trepidation, for I gathered that he would be of much the same character as several of the same class I had sorrowfully made acquaintance with before.

This is not the least of the sorrows which beset the poor, the manner in which their goods are distrained upon for a small debt, and furniture honestly worth twenty times the sum due is taken, and I was going to say sold—but it is never sold then, it is given away to a gang of heartless rogues, who make it their business to fatten upon the robbery of the poor within the law. In my case, however, there was no fear that they would take more than I owed. My furniture had cost me well over £100, and the two counters in the shop would easily have sold second-hand for £10, but I doubt if the whole of my chattels put together could, even if sold in a shop to the public, have been made to realise more than £30. It was not good furniture when I bought it, and though some of it was not now very old, it stood revealed as what it was, shoddy-built, of unseasoned wood, varnished instead of polished, upholstered with American cloth or sham velvet, and stuffed with unclassable rubbish.

My visitor arrived at about three o'clock, and to my relief he was quite a respectable and civil man. He quietly announced his errand as if it was a duty he was sorry to perform, and therefore I hastened to assure him that I could readily dissociate a man from his employment. Thus his work went on very smoothly, and was exceedingly soon over. Then he closed his book and turning to me said, " You haven't got much." I smiled wanly, and made no reply for obvious reasons. Then he went on to inform me that although he was an appraiser of the Court his inventory was only taken for the official purpose of checking the accounts of the firm to whom they would presently assign the task of dealing with it. And bade me a courteous good day, leaving me wishing that the whole degrading business was over.

Still I must say in strict justice that so far as it had gone, and remembering the immense number of formalities to be gone through, there had been scarcely any delay, but that I think was largely due to my personal interest in the matter and the energy I put into it. And now I was, all unknowing, come nearly to the end of the miserable business as far as my comfort and relief was concerned. I had one more quiet Sunday at the shop, spent in the usual way, and on Monday morning there arrived a man like a jovial costermonger of the better class out for a holiday— one of those men who are born comedians, whom to look at is to laugh, unless one is so sour or so sad that laughter is an impossibility. My very heart warmed to him, and when I found that he represented the firm of auctioneers, who were to deal with my chattels, I felt quite relieved, though I could not then have known any reason why I should be.

He was exceedingly abrupt and swift in all his movements, so that before I had realised that he had been through one room, he was beckoning me into the shop with a comic forefinger and an air of mystery. When I came up to him smiling in spite of myself, he said in a hoarse whisper, " Now, look y'ere, Guvnor, 'ow much yer goin' ter bid fer this little lot ? " and he bent his brows upon me in a funny frown. I stared at him blankly, and then stammered out, " I—I don't know what you mean." " Ow, you don't, don't yer. Well, I'll 'splaint yer. If I sen's one of our vans daown 'ere, and clears your sticks aht, we cawn't tike the trouble t' sell 'em orf bit by bit. 'Taint likely. Theyn't worf it. Nah, wot we sh'll do is ter sen rahnd t'one of ahr small Jew 'angers on, an' sye, ' Nah then, Moses or Abrams or Jyecob, as the kise mye be, wot yer givin' t' clear aht this little lot.' An' it's six ter four that we tikes 'is fust orfer, 'cause it don't matter t' us a bit on a little job like that, we gets the same commishun. Now, I mean that ter prevent that there kerlamity 'appenin' t'yer, you mike a bid for 'em yerself, an' you tike it strite from me that if your bid is anythin' over rubbish price ahr Guvnor 'll jump at it, syevin the trouble er tikin' it awye too an' all."

My brain, working furiously, had absorbed his whole meaning and exhausted every possible avenue of raising any more money by the time he had done speaking. And I shook my head, sadly murmuring, "It's no use. I'm most grateful to you for giving me this opportunity of saving my poor bits of goods, but I exhausted all my friend's means raising the money for the Court fees. I don't believe I could raise another sovereign to save my life." "P'raps not," returned he drily. "An' yet you might ter syve yer sticks. Nah once more, 'cause I got ter be movin', got arf dozen jobs on ter dye, you jist dig out like all possessed ter dye. Say you *will* 'ave a bit a brass ter sive that there poor little 'ome from bein' broke up, an' bring it, wotever it is, up t' th' orfice termorrow mornin' ten o'clock. I sh'll be there, an' I promise yer thet if it's anywheres near the mark the Guvnor 'll tike it. G'mornin,' keep yer chivvy up," and he was gone, whistling like a thrush, bless him.

While I stood there dazed, who should burst in, as was his custom, but my chum Bob from next door. I have said little of him lately, but indeed nothing could exceed the comfort that his cheery presence and sympathy had been all through this trying time. With money he could not help me, for he had but a very small salary, every penny of which he needed for the maintenance of his aged mother and himself; but he did what was even better at this time, he gave me himself, gave up such recreations as he had after his long day's confinement to come and talk over my lugubrious affairs, and try to devise ways of bettering them. Now he came up to me with a rush, saying,

" Hullo, old boy, how's things ? you look as if you'd had a knock."

Gratefully I turned to him, and in a few minutes he was in possession of the situation. He considered deeply for a little, and then said musingly, " I think I see a light. How many pictures have you got ready for sale ? I gave him the number," showed him the best of them, and he went on : " Will you let me try and sell 'em for you to-night, getting what I can for 'em ? " Of course I gladly acquiesced, as drowning men catch at straws, and salved my conscience for the dishonesty by the reflection that the transaction was really far more beneficial to my creditors, to say nothing of myself, than the clearing of them out by the Jew spoken of by my late visitor could possibly be.

" That's all right then," he said ; " now you get 'em all ready, an' as soon as I can get off, I'll trot 'em round." He secured leave from his duties, and began a circuit of his friends, and after making several visits to the shop for more pictures he came in at last about ten o'clock tired but triumphant, and slapped down £5. 19s. on the table. I felt so glad I had a bit of supper ready for him, as I had nothing to do but cook, for he was almost ravenous with hunger. With great glee, he recounted his experiences, how he had implored, cajoled, bullied, his friends into buying the pictures they had so long seen in my shop window, taking large discounts for ready money, but he did not tell

Q

me, nor did I discover until long afterwards, that he had borrowed nearly £2. 10s. of the money, and bought three pictures himself, for my sake, which he didn't want, and certainly could not afford. But then that was his idea of being a chum.

It was only now that I permitted myself to realise how wretched would have been my lot had it not been for those avenues of escape, illegal as they were. To have been stripped of every article of furniture, and turned with my young family into an empty house, with no credit, and without as far as I could see at present more than sufficient money than would buy the most necessary articles of food allowed me out of the wages I was earning, cannot be regarded in any other light than that of a severe penalty for being a bad business man. Yet such was the law, and it was only mitigated by evasion or defiance. There can, I think, be no doubt of the badness of the law which crushes those who obey it honestly, but permits itself to be rendered nugatory with the utmost ease and impunity by any who are sufficiently dishonest. Nay, more, which tacitly invites and fosters dishonesty and falsehood to such an extent that I am sure no decent man can ever go through the process of being made a bankrupt without having deep scars left in his soul.

But although my present relief was undoubtedly great, and I consequently felt much happier, I was by no means upon secure ground as yet. Therefore, I was exceedingly impatient when morning came to be off to the city with my precious little hoard. I was outside the office some time before the clock struck, and at the earliest possible moment I was inside, much to the disgust of the first arrivals, who resented my punctuality. My vivacious friend of the previous day was there, cutting jokes with all and sundry except me, whom he seemed to regard as a piece of furniture which had accidentally got left in the office, by which I gathered correctly that he did not want to be recognised by me.

Presently a clerk came towards me and said with a lowering face, "Who did you want to see?" I told him, the principal; upon which he disappeared into an inner office. When he returned, he said, "The Governor'll see you directly." Presently I was called in, and a very kindly old gentleman demanded my business. I told him I was a debtor upon whom his firm had orders to distrain, and that I had come up to make an offer to buy in my small stock of furniture, so small that it was hardly worth his while to remove. "Ah," he said, "you are Mr Bullen of Lordship Lane, I believe," consulting a book at his side. I answered that I was.

"Now then," he went on, "what are you prepared to bid for this furniture of yours?" "Five pounds," I replied as calmly as I could, though to tell the truth my heart was thumping with the excitement of the crisis. "Five pounds," he repeated scornfully, "for a houseful of furniture ! the thing's absurd. I never heard the like. Indeed you'll have to offer a good deal more than that." Very earnestly I answered him that it was quite impossible that I should do so. I had reached the limit, and that only by what I felt to be a miracle. Then he called the man whom I had received my instructions from, and consulted him in a low voice. The upshot of their conversation was that he turned to me and said, " My man here thinks your offer isn't out of the way, and so I'll accept it, but you must pay our fee." Again I assured him of my impecuniosity, but he cut me short by saying, " All right, you give me a promissory note to pay a guinea for my fee within a month, and the bargain's closed. But remember, if you try to chisel me, you'll be very sorry for it. My clerk will make out the receipt and note. He won't keep you waiting long."

So I paid the £5 and signed the promissory note. When I was leaving the office the principal said as if through an afterthought, " Look here, we've done with you—as far as we are concerned, your goods are free. But your landlord can distrain, if you let him, at any time between sunrise and sunset. So if I was you I'd shift those goods to another house— then they'll be safe and not before. Good morning."

It may be easily imagined what effect this advice had upon my already fretted nerves, and I felt as if I must fly. But when I got outside my friend was there, and I could do no less than thank him for his invaluable tip, succeeding at the same time in prevailing upon him to accept half-a-crown as a tiny recognition of, not payment for, his great kindness. Then I fled, suffering all the time until I reached home. I dashed into the shop where my wife was standing talking to Bob. I paid no attention to either of them, but seized the long arm, rushed outside, and began to pull the shutters down. " Whatever's the matter with you ? " cried my wife, and they both stared at me as if they thought I was mad. But I never heeded them until I had the place effectually closed, and then wiping my brow I turned to them and breathlessly declared the reason of my haste.

It is hardly to be wondered at that they both laughed until the tears ran down. I joined them after a while, but at the same time I had an overwhelming sense of danger passed. The rest of that day was devoted to preparations for moving, the new abode as I have before said having been secured. As soon as the legal limit of entry by bailiffs had passed, I sallied forth and hired a van, horse, and man, at one and sixpence an hour (see large bills), and the work of removal began. Of course Bob was in his element, and we worked liked demons. By supper-time we were fairly installed in the new premises and as comfortable as circumstances would permit. Nay, I am ungrateful, far more comfortable than I had been since I first took upon my unfit shoulders the burden of a shop.

The last duty I performed that night was to post to

the landlord the key of the premises with a line stating what it was. I did not add insult to injury by any expressions of apology, although I felt that an apology, very full and ample, was indicated. But, doubtless, the sense of exultation at having emerged from the late turmoil with my " bits of sticks," as the poor lovingly call their home plenishing, was uppermost in my mind, and overcame my sense of what was right and due to all, a tribute I was unable to pay. We had a delicious little supper of stewed rabbit and pickled pork that night, total cost for six eighteen-pence (because it was Monday, and Ostend rabbits unsold from Saturday were a little stale), and after-wards a long, long talk over the beginning of better times. Then we parted happily, and I enjoyed a perfect night's rest.

I had left in the shop the broken lamps, a few of the fittings and the two counters. I claim no credit for leaving those counters; they had cost me £10, but I could not have sold them on the spur of the moment for ten shillings, although they were legally mine, if the term can be used of transactions which all seemed to me extra-legal if not actually illegal. To tell the truth I detached the shop entirely from my mind; it was an incubus removed as was Christian's burden in the " Pilgrim's Progress," and, although never in the habit of making resolutions or swearing off, I felt that nothing could, would, or should ever induce me to take upon my shoulders such a burden again.

I went back to my office with a fairly light heart, except for the lingering doubts which always assailed me when I had been away a long time, and found everything proceeding calmly in its accustomed channels. I did learn afterwards that one kind gentleman, suffering from insufficiency of occupation, had brought my bankruptcy before the Secretary, and had been snubbed for his pains. The same philanthropist I afterwards learned had been to the manager of a firm to which I was indebted and suggested that they should get an order to garnishee my £2 a week, but was again repulsed in his benevolent ideas. I may say in passing that his salary was double mine, that he was a bachelor, and I was seven, like the Wordsworth child, and after that I think I can leave the matter.

How long it was after this sudden passing from storm to calm, before I was called upon to meet my creditors I do not know, but I do know that I woke every morning feeling that life had begun anew. The postman's knock (truly it was rare now) no longer gave me palpitation of the heart, nor did I fear that upon coming home, I should meet one of my uninvited guests with designs upon my " bits of sticks." Demands for money, peremptory, denunciatory, ceased automatically. I moved in a new world, where debts were not, and £2 a week was a neat little annuity amply sufficient for all present needs; and I began to feel again as if life was worth living. Of course I had carried my tools with me and had set up a bench where I might do an occasional job if the opportunity offered; and as many of my old customers sought me out, I still earned a little extra, which I found very useful.

When I had almost forgotten that such a place as the Bankruptcy Court existed, much less that I had ever owed any money, I received an order to attend a first meeting of creditors at the Court. Of course I attended promptly, but only one of my creditors appeared, and I learned afterwards that he only came for the purpose of opposing any hostile resolutions which might be proposed. There were none, and he said nothing, in fact the whole proceedings were of the most perfunctory nature and occupied less than a quarter of an hour. I saw my old friend Mr Hardhat, who congratulated me upon the smooth way in which my affairs were going. "Now," he said, "there's only the public examination, and as soon as that is over you can apply for your discharge." I thanked him, and paid him the very small sum in which he said I was indebted to him, went away, and in another fortnight forgot the shameful business again.

The thought, however, would continually arise in my mind, how very different my position was now compared to what it had been a few days ago. Then, while fighting most desperately against overwhelming odds to pay my way and do my duty, I was being literally harassed to death; now, having by a substantial payment, not to my creditors but to the Government, obtained the right to declare my inability to pay anybody, I was left in perfect peace, and even in my appointed meeting with creditors no man of all those to whom I owed money came to say a word against me. I was not at all inclined to question very closely the means by which I had obtained deliverance from the morass in which I had so long been floundering, but the reflections would continually obtrude themselves, and I could only say with a sigh, as so many others have said in a like case, that it was a topsy-turvy world.

Then came the day of my public examination, but it had no terrors for me, for I knew that it could make no difference to me now, and besides I rather welcomed the opportunity of saying something in public on my own behalf. But I little thought that I was to have an object lesson in the absurdity and injustice of our Bankruptcy laws that day which would dwell in my mind as long as I lived. Yet it was so, and although I have read of many more flagrant instances since they are only exaggerations of this case, the principle is the same.

A man was being examined whose salary and commission had for over twenty years been more than £1200 a year. His debts were over £5000, contracted in all sorts of extravagant ways, and his creditors were very angry indeed. Now his assets were nil— I heard nothing about the selling up of his home or of his being turned out of the house for which he was supposed to pay £100 a year rent. In reply to questions he pleaded that he had a large family, but it turned out that the eldest was twenty-five and the youngest fourteen. Asked what reason he could assign for being in this position, he could or would give none but living beyond his means. Then came the very pertinent question, what did he propose to do ?

Well, in the first place, said his eminent solicitor, his employers were willing to retain him in their service providing that he obtained his discharge, but not otherwise. Supposing that to be the case, his earnings would be much reduced, say to £800 a year. Now the proposition made was that whatever he earned over £600 a year should be set aside to be distributed *pro rata* among his creditors until they had received a dividend of five shillings in the pound on their claims. All this on condition only that he received his discharge then and there. There was some little talk, purely I judged for the sake of appearances, and then he was discharged to begin again. Now I do not say that this was injustice, but if it was just, what was I to call the treatment I subsequently received ?

I was presently subjected to a searching examination by a very clever gentleman, who dilated upon my iniquity in continuing to trade after I knew that I was unable to fulfil my obligations. All the questions put were from the notes of my preliminary examination, and I felt very grateful for my excellent memory.

No creditor appeared to say a word in my disfavour, and the examination was concluded, nothing apparently having been done for or against me. I was puzzled, and as soon as I got outside the Court I eagerly enquired of my faithful Mr Hardhat, who was waiting for me, what I ought to do now. "Apply for your discharge at once," said he, "for if you delay it, the period you will be suspended for (and it's sure to be two years), will only date from the time of application, however long hence that may be." Of course I was eager to apply at once, but when I learned that there would be more fees to pay amounting to several pounds, none of which money would benefit my creditors at all, I indignantly refused to do anything of the sort, and said that I didn't care if I was never discharged, I would pay no more fees if I had thousands. And I rejoice to say that I never did.

# CHAPTER XVII

## THE DAY DAWNS

THE emphatic declaration I made at the end of the last chapter seems to demand an explanation forthwith, but the reader, if he has had patience to follow me so far in my recital of these experiences, must wait for the proper sequence of events. Being assured that I was absolutely free from molestation by anybody on account of past debts, and in no danger of any trouble so long as I did not obtain credit to the extent of £20 without disclosing the fact that I was an undischarged bankrupt, I went on my way rejoicing. For whatever doubts I had about my future, of one thing I was certain, and that was that I would never go into business again as a tradesman, and as for getting credit for £20 I laughed at the idea.

Perhaps I was too elated at the knowledge that I was free from the hateful incubus which had robbed me of all joy in my life for so long, but I think I had some excuse, and whether I had or not I allowed myself to feel happy. Occasionally I felt depressed by the thought of how near I was to forty years of age, how small were my chances of starting my children in life, and how tired and worn out I was feeling, but I was naturally elastic of temperament, and the rebound I had lately felt was entirely beneficial to me. I worked at the bench still, but with reluctance, because I had learned by bitter experience, that work I never so hard, the reward was entirely incommensurate with the outlay of energy. And so I took less and less interest in picture framing, and got back again to my beloved books in greater measure than ever.

Also I scribbled more and got several articles accepted at long intervals, the remuneration for which, though pleasant to receive and always coming in handy to meet some most pressing need, such as clothes for the children, never raised in me any hopes of a permanent and substantial addition to my income. For I still regarded, by some twist of mind, the picture framing as my stand-by, although one article which I could write in an evening or in the morning before going to work would yield more when sold than I could earn in a week's overtime by the really hard work of framing, to say nothing of the labour involved in fetching the material and carrying home the finishing product. Not that I ever received any extravagant prices for my writing. With one honourable exception, *Chambers's Journal*, all the organs I wrote for seemed anxious to get what I wrote for the smallest possible sum, or nothing if I could be made to forget that they had published my stuff. To one journal with an august name and a large circulation, having also an advertisement revenue of many thousands a year, I sent a story of 5000 words. I received a most courteous letter in reply with a statement that while they would much like to print the story, which was an excellent one, they could only offer me ten shillings for it! I took it, never mind why.

But taking things all round I was happier than I had been for many a day. Having been set free from that awful burden of the shop, and being finished for ever, (I hoped) with the whole body of County Court officials, bum-bailiffs, etc., I experienced a restful peace to which I had long been a stranger. I recovered much of my lost vigour, for although the habit of work still clung to me and I did not waste a minute if I could help it, I no longer dreaded a knock at the door, no longer felt symptoms of heart failure at the sight of a postman coming towards me. Now and then I thought of my fortieth birthday fast approaching, believing as I did that a man of forty was too old to strike out any new line, that if he had never done anything worth doing he never would, and much more of the same tenor. But most happily, however these pessimistic thoughts harassed me they did not affect my conduct, not because I determined that they should not, or braced myself in an heroic resolve to defy fate, age, or anything else that should tend to hinder my advancement, but for the same reason that I kept going so long in that hopeless shop, because the necessity was laid upon me, as the nigger song says, to keep " a-pushin' an' a-shovin'." Very disagreeable to other people in many cases this persistence of a fellow for whom *they* cannot see the slightest necessity, but then, so much depends upon the point of view.

My only object in writing the penultimate sentence is to clear myself of any suspicion of false hypocritical pretence. I have the greatest horror and detestation of posing as one who, by sheer force of will and decision of character, has conquered circumstances, lived instead of died, and although wrecked apparently beyond salvage has reconstructed something navigable and sailed away from a far more profitable voyage. For I know that these things depend upon the quality of the fibre of which a man is wrought and for which he can take no credit. It is this which often keeps a man at work when, had he been living in more prosperous conditions, he would have been in bed with grave doctors and nurses around him, and hourly bulletins as to his temperature, etc., being issued. I remember during the first influenza epidemic the case of a carter for one of the great carrying companies in London who, it being a busy season, had been on duty twenty hours. He drove into the yard in the small hours of the morning, dropped the reins on his horse's back, but did not descend from his dickey. As he gave no reply to repeated hailing by his mates below, one mounted to him and found him stiff in death. It came out at the inquest that on leaving home twenty hours before he had told his wife that he felt very bad, one moment shivering and the next burning, and all his limbs one big ache, but the fibre of the man insisted upon going on. Fear of losing his job, of being short in his scanty week's earnings had spurred him, but the frame gave out under the great strain put upon it by the spirit.

You may call it heroism if you will, but if it has any of that sublime quality I am sure it is unconscious, innate, and not to be referred to any conceived and determined desire to overcome obstacles apparently insurmountable. Of course it is far more admirable, more worthy of respect than is the conduct of the weakling who wilts under the first blast of adversity, who must always be bolstered up and pushed along the way that he ought to go, and never does anything for himself that he can get others to do for him—a born loafer, in fact, for whom there really is no room in a work-a-day world, but who, alas! thrives bodily upon the labours of others, and is often treated with far more consideration than those who are steadily labouring on.

It was about this time that I unconsciously dropped upon a new form of activity entirely aloof from the tradesman line. I was a worker in a humble little mission whereof none of the members earned more than £2 a week, and some only half that sum. I had joined it in my desire to get away from the cabals and jealousies of the ordinary church or chapel where two-thirds of the good that might be done is wasted

upon most unchristian friction between members. I
had got thoroughly disgusted with them all as far as
my experience had gone, and I felt that my only hope
of remaining associated with a body of Christians was
to get as low down as possible, where nobody could
put on side or ape the patron.

Now it was our custom in our little hall during the
winter months to give, whenever we could raise
sufficient funds, a free tea to the poor neglected
children of the neighbourhood, of whom there were a
sad number. It always meant a lot of work collecting
the few shillings necessary, but that work was never
grudged by any of us, and we always felt sufficiently
rewarded at the sight of the poor kiddies stuffing
themselves. How cheaply we did it to be sure. Tea
never cost us more than one shilling a pound, condensed
milk, threepence halfpenny a pound tin; good cake,
from the philanthropic firm of Peek Frean, we got for
fourpence, and sometimes threepence a pound; and
other matters, including margarine, on a like scale.
Oh, it was a feast! and there was always a hungry
crowd of grown-ups outside at the close who were
grateful for the carefully saved fragments.

Well! it came to pass that at this particular time
I speak of the winter promised to be exceptionally
severe, and we could not raise funds for our free teas.
So, in a moment of inspiration, I suggested that if we
could raise sufficient funds to have some lantern slides
made from pictures which I would get, and take the

R

Peckham Public Hall, I would give a lecture on the South Sea Whaling industry, of which I had never forgotten a detail. All the brethren entered into the proposal *con amore*, but I doubt if it would ever have matured but for a recent convert, a young clerk in a big manufacturing house, who drew out his savings and financed the affair.

That difficulty over, we went ahead full speed and pestered everybody we knew to buy tickets, getting a guinea by the way from Sir John Blundell Maple, who probably thought it was worth that to shelve us when we applied to him for his patronage of the show. The great night arrived, and we had secured a popular local preacher to take the chair. His organist had promised to play an accompaniment for two sacred songs which I was to sing, and best of all, four hundred tickets were sold. Our popular preacher, however, very nearly ruined us, for, after introducing me in a very graceful speech, he said to my shame and indignation, " Will brother so-and-so lead us in prayer," naming a long-winded old donkey who would ramble you on for an indefinite length of time in a babblement that was anything but prayer, even if such a prologue was at all indicated on such an occasion.

I verily believe that I lost a pint of sweat while that old idiot maundered on. I felt in every nerve the impatience and disgust of the mixed audience, and at last, in despair, I actually prayed myself that the Lord would stop his wretched twaddle, for it was nothing else. Apparently my prayer was answered, almost immediately, for he had a violent paroxysm of coughing which enabled us to go ahead. Of course I was not at all nervous, my long training in the open air prevented that, and equally of course (I suppose) the strangeness of the subject held the suburban folk enthralled. However that may have been, I know that presently seeing my last slides appearing and fearing that I was cutting the matter too short, I asked a friend of mine in front (in a stage whisper) the time. "Ten o'clock, Tom," he promptly replied, in a voice audible all over the hall. My, but there was nearly a panic. Some wise person turned the lights up, and in about two minutes nearly everybody had gone.

You see, divers of them came from far, and our Peckham communications in those days were none of the best. A few faithful local ones remained till the bitter end however, and my superintendent, who was a chimney-sweep, said in broken accents from the platform, swabbing his eyes meanwhile, " I never knoo we 'ad sich a bruvver ! " And what more in the way of commendation and honest praise could the heart of man desire than that ? Only this, that the net profits of the lecture, after all expenses were paid, were £14 all but a shilling or two, a far greater sum than we had ever had before to spend upon free teas for poor children.

Then, at the instigation of a lantern fiend, I beg the dear chap's pardon, a lantern enthusiast, who offered his services and his truly exquisite set of slides free, I gave a series of four lectures on the life of Christ in the little hall itself. A blind performer on the organ flutina, who knew nearly all the classic hymns by heart, was easily secured at the economical figure of half a crown per evening, and I interspersed my remarks with all the old favourite hymns, that now are indeed caviare to the general, sung solo. Such an entertainment as I then gave, which of course would be impossible to me now, would, I am sure, bring me in twenty guineas a night. For I could sing and I could talk, the pictures and the music were alike excellent but—. The total net produce was about fifteen shillings for four nights! There, it's the first bit of brag I've given utterance to in the course of these chapters, and this is its fitting anti-climax.

But if I did not receive much for my services as far as money went, either for myself or the cause, I did gain invaluable experience in addressing indoor audiences. I was already thoroughly at home with any crowd in the open air, but I found that it was a totally different matter to speak inside a building, even to the method of producing the voice and sustaining it without obvious effect or real fatigue for a couple of hours if need arose. And as I had previously discovered in the open air that straining the voice ranting or raving was not only indicative of insincerity but precluded intelligibility as well, so, in a renewed and more definite sense, I found it here, and I am beyond measure grateful for that experience. For I hate to hear a speaker, on whatever subject, yell or shout at his audience as if he had a personal quarrel with every one of them, just as much as I hate mannerisms of any kind on the platform, regarding them all as a sort of showing off that is only worthy of a pampered child.

The upshot of this practice at home, as I might say, was that I began to get a local reputation as a lecturer, and any struggling church or chapel in the neighbourhood trying to raise funds would give me a cordial invitation to come and help them, providing my own lanternist, etc., for the good of the cause; and for a time I went, unconscious that I was by way of being a blackleg, but exceedingly conscious that the *silver* collections asked for on these occasions were mostly copper with a goodly sprinkling of farthings. In my natural modesty (the reader may laugh quietly at this but I can assure him that the possession of this quality, so beautiful in women, is in excess entirely detrimental to man, since the world takes us largely at our own valuation), I felt that these meagre results were a sufficient guage of my popularity.

Still I did remember occasionally, to my comfort, a small experience I had once, in Portland, Oregon. Three of us common sailors were invited to a Methodist Episcopal Church to hear a lecture, by a phenomenal preacher, entitled, " The Life, Death, and Resurrection of an Arab." We were almost appalled by the magnificence of the place, which, for luxury of appointment, could give points to any place of public entertainment I have ever been in. Silk velvet lounges for pews, upholstered like feather beds, soft Turkey carpets on the floor, hammered brass enrichments to the carven woodwork—the place reeked of wealth. At the close of the lecture the preacher went round with his own top hat for the collection, in his humility not desiring any help from the church officers. And the result in spot cash, as they would say, was four dollars and ninety-two cents! of which our party might have been credited with ten cents. A widow's mite indeed, for it was all we had. Able seamen ashore in a foreign port, except on liberty day, rarely have any money, and I am sure I don't know why we had that solitary dime. But the lesson of the affair was that services, however valuable in themselves, rendered gratis, or in the hope that the audience will be generous, are usually taken by the recipients as not worth recognising. The higher the price the performer can charge and get, the more he or she is appreciated. It is a fact never to be forgotten.

Thus it came about that I did not get puffed up by any roseate visions of becoming a popular lecturer—how could I when I had seen an audience of eight hundred yield fourteen shillings and elevenpence three farthings? But I had a solid asset always in the glow of satisfaction that I could address a big crowd and interest them, a pleasure which was hardly clouded even for a moment by such remarks as I heard a burly man make once in a chapel at Peckham where I was lecturing. In a hoarse whisper he said to a neighbour, " What's this 'ere all about, Guvnor ? " " Whales," replied his interlocutor. " Ho, is it ? " he growled. " Well, s'rimps is more in my line or winkles. 'Ere, let me get aht ! "

Almost imperceptibly I was dropping my picture framing connection. Much as I had enjoyed the work, apart from the struggle to add to my income by it, I had grown to hate it from its associations. That none of the men who had trusted me with their goods had even so much as appeared against me when I had figured as a bankrupt under examination only made me feel grateful to them, it did not lessen my horrors of the means by which I had been brought to the sad pass I had so lately emerged from. And so as I did not pursue the business with any energy it gradually fell away, and I was not in the least sorry, although I had not got to the point yet of refusing any work that came in my way.

But I had grown quite unconsciously into the habit of writing, had become used to seeing what I had written in print even to the point of wondering not what the world would think of it, but what the editor would think it worth while to pay me for it. Also I had grown to be infected by the spirit of adventure, common to most literary men. By which I mean that, unlike the tradesman, who, with a steady demand for his goods, which people must have, fixes his profits with due regard to the practice of his competitors, and does not dream of vicissitudes, they must always reckon upon a change in the public taste or in the idiosyncrasies of editors. It is a sportsmanlike feeling, and I must say that it appealed to me very strongly as a pastime, but I always regarded the cheques which I received as a gift from on high. When I got an article or story accepted, I rejoiced and was exceedingly glad, and then I endeavoured to forget all about it. Because I never knew what I was going to get, nor when I was going to receive it. Therefore when it came it was in the nature of a find. Needless to say, I always wanted it very badly, and always wondered whatever I should have done without it, but that I think only added to my joy.

Then came an opportunity which I thought but little of, at that time, but have since seen the importance of. An article appeared in a scientific journal of high standing upon a subject which I had made peculiarly my own, and about which I had the most intimate personal knowledge. A friend brought this article to my notice, and I, feeling amazed at its assumptions, wrote to the editor about it. As a result he requested me to write an article for him on the matter, and I did so. Now, having regard to the standing of the journal in question, and the fact that I had been invited to write, I broke my rule of non-expectancy, and looked for a substantial reward. Alas for my hopes. The article duly appeared—it was well over four thousand words, and in three months I received for it thirty-seven and sixpence! I regard that now as I regarded it then, an outrage. Yet I suppose that is really how men of science are paid in this country.

I am happy to say that I have never written for a scientific journal since, and I put that experience by the side of the other which I mentioned before as being parallel cases and warnings. Why, many a provincial newspaper struggling for a bare existence would have paid a hack writer more. But few people outside the charmed circle know how shamefully certain journals with an immense advertisement revenue exploit the poor scribes who fill their columns of reading matter with the fine fruit of brains and experience.

There is another curious little matter connected with this, which is entirely germane, and I think it of considerable interest, which I should like to mention as a particular instance. At one of our seaport towns I met with a man in Government employ, whose pay was at the rate of about £100 a year, but who possessed ability and mathematical qualifications of a very high order. In the course of conversation with him one day I learned that he had contributed over sixty articles, in the space of two years, to at least a dozen different daily and weekly journals. Some of these articles were 3000 words in length, and none were under a thousand. Many of them had been printed in prominent places, and were obviously considered by the editors as of great importance, as indeed they were. When I had glanced through some of them I said cheerfully, " I am very glad that you have been able to add to your scanty income in this way ; it should lead to something very lucrative in time." " Oh," he replied, quite innocently, " I have never received anything for them. I thought that they weren't worth paying for."

I was astounded for a moment, and then asking him for a piece of paper, I drafted him a form of account to send to each of those journals. He did so, and in a week's time I was delighted to receive a grateful letter from him saying that my little bit of advice had resulted in his getting £60. He added that it would probably save the life of his dear wife, who had been ordered away by the doctor, advice impossible for him to follow before owing to lack of means. Well, heaven knows the remuneration he received was little enough, but it was better than nothing. What a condition of things when concerns yielding huge fortunes to their owners will stoop so low as to allow poor men to give them of their best, and never offer a halfpenny in return until dunned for it, and then only on so niggardly a scale.

I cannot close this chapter without saying that this practice is by no means universal, but it is decidedly general. I have myself been begged by an editor, yes, literally begged, to write an article for a pittance so small that I am ashamed to say I accepted it; and found afterwards that the article in question had been sold to several other journals for a big profit!

# CHAPTER XVIII

## THE JOY OF SUCCESS

NOW from the foregoing chapter it will be gathered that all unconsciously I was drifting into the habit of writing, in a literary and journalistic sense, for payment. It was a timid and tentative sort of beginning, and I often felt the rewards totally inadequate, especially in the matter of newspaper paragraphs, of which I sent out a good number. But my efforts in this direction suddenly received a most unexpected and gratifying fillip. Glancing one day in the Free Library through the columns of the Illustrated London News, I discovered, with a pleasant feeling at the pit of the stomach, as if I had just imbibed something warm and stimulating, that Dr Andrew Wilson, that genial kindly journalist and lecturer, had devoted his weekly column to my scientific article, allusion to which was made at the close of the last chapter.

I need not now record what he said, but it was so kindly and helpful that I began to feel a strange sensation—that of hope. For I could not help thinking that if what I wrote was worthy of the attention of so able a critic and journalist, it ought to be saleable generally. And so I wrote him a grateful letter, and asked him if he would follow up his kindness by introducing me to the editors of some of the journals for which he wrote, imagining in my ignorance that to be writing regularly for a paper or magazine argued not merely acquaintance with the editor, but influence over his acceptance of articles. I have since found that it is a very general misapprehension. As if the fact of a man being chosen to be editor of a publication did not prove that in the estimation of his employers at least he was capable of independent judgment, and might be relied upon to exercise it !

The jolly doctor answered me very promptly and kindly, but firmly disabused my mind of the idea that he had any influence with editors. In fact he told me, what, if I had possessed any knowledge of the profession at all I might have known, that editors rather resented any attempt on the part of a contributor to introduce other people. He advised me, as Kipling did later, to send my stuff in on its unaided merit, and suggested " Longmans' " and the " Cornhill " as two likely magazines to appreciate my matter. I wrote and thanked him, went home and got out a four thousand word article and posted it to the editor of "Longmans'," enclosing a stamped addressed envelope, for I had learned that much anyhow. The article was entitled, " Some Incidents of the Sperm Whale Fishery," and as I now know, would not in the least appeal to Mr

Andrew Lang.. I got it returned almost immediately, with the usual printed slip expressing the editor's regret, etc. Of course, I felt disheartened, having some indefinite idea that the advice I had received from Dr Andrew Wilson had more in it than struck the ear.

There was still left the "Cornhill," though, and being unwilling to risk the loss of the postage I walked across the park to the office of that pleasant publication, and laid my contribution upon the ledge devoted to correspondence. As the sequel has been made public property, by that kindly gentleman and good friend of mine, Mr J. St Loe Strachey, who was then Editor of the "Cornhill," I have no hesitation in reproducing it here. At that time the "Cornhill," like so many other magazines, was suffering from a plethora of accepted MSS., and Mr Strachey had accordingly given instructions to his assistant, Mr Roger Ingpen, not to give him any more MSS. to look at even, since none could possibly be accepted for a very long time. But Mr Ingpen is an extremely conscientious and careful man ; he is withal of a most kindly disposition, and so it came about that my poor MS., instead of being returned unread with a statement of the cause, was carefully looked through. In the result Mr Ingpen handed it to Mr Strachey with a remark that here was something so fresh, and in his opinion so good, that he would not take the responsibility of returning it until his chief had seen it. Mr

Strachey uttered some expression of impatience, but thrust the MS. into his pocket, and read it on his way home. And, lest I should become wearisome, it appeared in the earliest possible number of the magazine.

It was, all unknown to me, a momentous time. The acceptance of that MS. changed the whole course of my life. For if it had been returned from the " Cornhill," for whatever reason might have been assigned, I had determined to destroy it, as prior to sending it to " Longmans'," it had been rejected by the Editor of " Answers " (who wrote me a note about my folly in sending such stuff to a journal of the high character of " Answers "), and by the editor of " Chambers' Journal." So I felt justified in assuming that if the " Cornhill " would have none of it the verdict must be final—it was no good. And yet upon how many little things its acceptance hung! The fact of Mr Ingpen's care and appreciation, of my really good and clear handwriting without which Mr Strachey certainly would not have read it, it being his custom never to read MSS. if he can possibly avoid doing so. And then there is that unknown contributor whose story was displaced to make room for mine —how I hope that he was some renowned person to whom the non-appearance of his stuff made no difference !

When the article appeared it in some manner caught the eye, and appealed to the taste, of Mr W. T.

Stead, who had then started the " Review of Reviews."
He gave it a lengthy notice, in the course of which he
stated his opinion that I had struck a new vein of
stirring adventure which should prove a very valuable
one. Encouraged by reading this, I wrote to Mr
Stead, telling him that I had partly written a book
upon the lines of my article, and begging his advice
as to getting it published, for I told him I knew
nothing about the publishing world, and had an idea
that unless a new writer had *influence* (whatever
I supposed that to be), he stood no chance of getting
anything published except by paying for it. And I,
so far from being able to pay money for having a book
published, was extremely anxious to earn some by the
sale of my writings.

In his reply, which was prompt and kindly, he
recommended me to Messrs Smith, Elder & Co., the
publishers of the " Cornhill," assuring me that no
introduction was necessary, that all publishers were
always on the lookout for new writers, and that if
my book was as good as the sample he thought I need
have no doubt of its acceptance. So upon this advice
I wrote to Messrs Smith, Elder & Co., offering to submit
the portion of the book I had already written (some
50,000 words) for their approval. Naturally they
suggested I should finish the book first, and then they
would be delighted to consider it, and give me their
decision as early as possible. Thus encouraged I
toiled early and late to finish the book, and when I

had done so I submitted it to Messrs Smith, Elder, who almost immediately accepted it. But the story has often been told, and I would rather not repeat myself if possible. I only tell what I have about it in order to lead up to something else which belongs to this book, to these confessions, an echo of the dreadful time through which I had passed. I may say, however, that had I been a superstitious man, I should certainly have felt that my success in getting my first book accepted and the, to me, immense sum of £100 paid me for it, was dearly purchased by a terrible domestic blow. Hitherto, in spite of much illness and privation in my family, its circle had remained intact. Now, however, with the first gleam of prosperity that I had ever known in all my life, came the grim shadow of death. On the day that I received the letter of acceptance of my book, my youngest child, a boy of great promise and beautiful disposition, suddenly died. Mercifully I had a tremendous amount of work on hand that week. I had quite a large order for picture frames to execute, the last by the way that I ever did. I had to remove from one house to another, to attend to the burial business, and to do my office work also. Therefore I had no time to think until all was well over, and the tragedy had become only a sad memory.

This marked a turning point in my career which led to some amazing results. I had hitherto never seemed able to do anything right, now I could do

s

nothing wrong. Orders for literary work flowed in upon me, and when the book was published the critics vied with one another in the kindliness of their remarks. Everyone seemed bent upon trying to turn my head. That, however, was impossible, for, in the first place, I was past forty years of age, and in the next my training in the school of adversity had been too long and thorough to permit of my being puffed up now. Of course I began to save money, and as soon as I did my thoughts turned to those friendly creditors of mine who had behaved with such wonderful leniency to me in the day of my trouble. My old German creditor especially I remembered. Now after I had become bankrupt I still went to his warehouse to buy my materials, and always stole in and out like a thief ashamed to meet him, but one day did so. He said, with a queer smile, " So, Meesder Bullen, you vas all right now, hein ! ve dont makes no trouble for you, hein ! now you soon bicks opp agen, hein ! but tondt go buyin' your mouldins someveres ellas now mit your ready money, gome here all de time. Ve makes you righdt. Cood day."

Of this good old man, and the others not less kind, I now thought continually, and as I reckoned up my savings week by week my hopes grew stronger that I should soon be able to pay all my debts. As they did so, I made a resolve that if I ever did become able to pay those obligations my creditors should receive every penny I had to give, not a doit should be impounded by bankruptcy officials. For I knew and hated the system whereby a bankrupt's estate has an immense amount of it swallowed up in the costs of division. Of course I know that the machinery of a great concern like the Court of Bankruptcy needs funds to carry it on, but I am perfectly sure that the costs in which the creditors are mulcted are enormously in excess of what they should rightly be.

Therefore I determined that when I had accumulated sufficient funds to satisfy all my debts I would give myself the great pleasure of going to each creditor personally, and paying him what I owed him. Then when all were paid I would take the receipted bills to the Court, and demand to be discharged from being a bankrupt. That was my programme, but like many another well laid plan it did not work. As you shall see.

When at last the time arrived so eagerly waited for, and I had about £400 saved, I took a day's leave from the office (I was soon to leave it altogether), and going to the Court hunted up my old and tried friend, Mr Hardhat. Giving him a substantial fee for taking him away from the Court, we adjourned to a neighbouring hotel, where I unfolded my plan to him. He listened attentively until I had finished, and then said judicially, " Yes, it's all very well and honest and all the rest of it, but if you will excuse my saying so it's very foolish. In the first place every one of your creditors has wiped your account off his books as a bad debt, and you'll hardly get thanks for re-opening the matter, even though you come with the money in your hand. In the next you'll certainly get into trouble with the Court for not proceeding in the matter regularly, and you may be sure they will suspend your discharge for as long as they possibly can. The four years which has elapsed your bankruptcy will not be reckoned. What you ought to do is to take half the sum you have mentioned, go to the Official Receiver, and tell him that a friend has offered to pay that sum into Court in consideration of you getting your immediate discharge, and all will go through like clock-work."

I waited very impatiently until he had finished, because I knew beforehand all the facts he was telling me, and then I said grimly, "And how much of that £200 do you suppose my creditors will get by the time it has filtered through the Court?" He smiled and murmured abstractedly, "I'd rather not say." "Well," I went on, "my mind is made up. Every penny that I have saved up to pay my debts with shall go to the people I owe the money to, and I'll do the distribution most gladly. I paid £10 in Court fees almost with my heart's blood, and they'll get no more if I can help it." I had forgotten to mention that being unable to redeem the beautiful piano in time it was lost, and the pawnbroker got for £8 an instrument honestly worth £40.

So we parted the best of friends, and I with my cheque-book in my pocket began my happy journey.

I wish with all my heart that I was able to give you some idea of the joy I had that day and the next. As nothing had ever given me greater pain, shame and humiliation, than having to make excuses for not paying money which I legally owed, as the degradation of borrowing had eaten into my very soul, so now the exultation of being able to clear myself, as it were, was correspondingly great. I verily believe that was the happiest (consciously the happiest) day of all my life. And I was asked to surrender all that delight to some cold-blooded official, who would exact an enormous toll for the services rendered by his department. The very thought of 'such a thing was preposterous. It would have been literally flinging away the joy which I had anticipated so long and so eagerly.

The first man that I called upon was a mount-cutter, who had a small business in which he worked very hard himself. I owed him £12, an amount which he certainly could ill afford to lose, but which he had been obliged to regard as hopelessly gone. He was an exceedingly kind and genial man, and one with whom I had been on most intimate terms, so that my pain and grief at letting him in had been very great. I greeted him cordially, and said, " Mr ——, I have come to pay you that money I owe you, and I cannot say how glad I am to be able to do it. I believe it is £12." And with that I got out my cheque-book. He stared at me for a moment, and then replied in a strained voice, " I am so glad, not merely of the money, though it could not be more welcome than it is to-day, when I have just learned of a loss of £50, money lent to help a friend, but because you have come spontaneously to pay me. It does me very much good in every way, gives me a little better opinion of human nature, and I thank you most heartily." I wrote out the cheque and handed it to him, saying what I knew to be the absolute truth, that it could not give him more pleasure to receive his just due than it gave me to be able and willing to pay it. Then I told him of the happy turn of fortune which had enabled me to do this act of justice and honesty, and he listened delightedly. We then shook hands, and parted both with a glow of good feeling that was priceless.

Then with eager steps I hastened to the warehouse of my old German creditor, but alas I found that he was dead. It was a heavy blow, for I had so looked forward to seeing him without a downcast eye and a shrinking sense of dishonesty. His successor in the business accepted my cheque in the most matter-of-fact way, making no comment. But that affected me not at all, although I came away less springily than I did from the first creditor.

Then I made my way to the establishment of a big Jewish firm to whom I owed a considerable sum for fancy goods on my wife's side of the business. The manager, a wonderfully able business man with a bright incisive manner, remembered me at once, but said directly I mentioned my errand, "Oh, but that's all settled and done with. You went through the Court, didn't you?" "Yes," I replied, "but that didn't cancel my obligation. It was only a temporary expedient, and now that I am able to pay I want to do so." "Oh, very well," he rejoined carelessly, "we'll turn it up." So the books were brought. He looked up the matter, and turning to me with an air of surprise, exclaimed, "But this has nothing to do with you. It's in your wife's name!" I laughed and answered, "Yes, I know that, but it's my debt all the same, and I want to pay it."

It may sound incredible, but it is nevertheless true, that I had quite a difficulty in persuading that gentleman to take my cheque, for he kept protesting that it was no affair of mine. Even after I had handed the cheque to him, he held it towards me and said, "It's not too late you know, take it back; you've no need to pay this." And when I laughingly refused to do anything of the sort he said, with a shrug of his shoulders, "Well, you're a fool, of course, but you're a damned good sort of a fool, and if you'll accept my invitation I'll give you the best dinner that can be got in the city of London for money. I look upon you as a natural curiosity." Gleefully I assured him that dinners, except as a necessary means of keeping the machine going, never troubled me, that I had grown to like only the plainest food, and that in very small quantities. But I hastened to assure him that I nevertheless valued his kindly intention as highly as if I had been a gourmet. So *we* parted, and I have never seen him since.

From thence I went to another city house to which I owed a substantial sum. Here, however, I had never seen the principal, my dealings having been entirely through the traveller who called upon me, and who I have no doubt had been in serious trouble through my failure. My business here was of the most formal nature, for the cashier had nothing to do with the previous course of the business, only to receive my payment and to give me a quittance. But the sequel to this was perhaps the most surprising of all those eventful experiences. The next day I received a letter from the principal of the firm couched in the most charming terms. He had discovered he said that I was the writer of certain books, the reading of which had given him the greatest pleasure of that kind he had ever known. It was exceedingly difficult, he went on, to realise that I was the struggling trades-man whom he had so often caused to be harassed for the amount of his account; had he known who it was he would certainly not have troubled me. And now, as the only reparation he was able to make for what he felt had been his harshness towards me, he begged to return the cheque (I believe it was for £35), which nothing could induce him to accept. And he begged to wish me all possible happiness and prosperity as well as long life to go on giving pleasure.

I only wish I could add to my present pleasure by

giving this good man's name, but that, alas, is out of the question for obvious reasons. But does not such an experience as this give one an exalted sense of the kindliness, courtesy, and active benevolence, that is to be found among business men. My motives in writing this book may be variously assessed, but I feel that I am only discharging an obvious duty in putting on record so fragrant, so elevating a record of fact. It should give persons inclined to cynicism a better, higher idea of their fellows. For it cannot be supposed that my experiences were unique, that I was specially singled out for such treatment. No, I believe that in every walk of life the good, the real good, in man far outweighs the evil, and that it is an entirely false and narrow view which sees in every man you do business with one whose mission in life is to *do* everybody he can, caring for nobody but himself. And I seek no better proof than that of my own experience.

Occasionally the honest kindly fair dealing trader or private person will be *done*, will be swindled ruthlessly. Now and then one comes across a man who simply lives to do harm, whose gall of envy is such that he will take any mean advantage to ruin another man whom he envies, even though in the process he only injures himself. Thank God, these are the exceptions, not the rule. On the contrary, in the good old way these exceptions only prove the rule that love, justice, and mercy are general, and that hatred, injustice, and cruelty are only sad upheavals of devilishness which are gradually but surely growing less and less able to harm well-doing folk.

Pleasant as these experiences were, and gratefully as I cherish them, I do not think that they were more so than some later ones, when I sought out some old friends who had lent me money to help me out of my constantly recurring difficulties, knowing full well when they did so that the chances of getting repaid were exceedingly slight.  One of these friends indeed was a Swiss to whom in the early days of our friendship I had rendered some slight assistance in his endeavour to get arrears of four years wages from his employer, a compatriot who had been exploiting him on the ground of his ignorance of England and her ways. From him I learned how wonderfully these toiling Swiss managed to save.  His wages never exceeded thirty shillings a week, out of which I should say, I never knew exactly, he saved seventy-five per cent. At any rate he was able to live for four years without receiving any wages from his employer, sleeping in a greenhouse at night (they were gardeners), and eating God knows what.

I met him at the mission with which I was associated in Paddington, and seeing his friendlessness asked him to my humble home for Sunday dinner and tea. And thus our friendship grew and ripened until I was able to render him the service aforesaid, thinking as I did that he was on the verge of starvation.  To my intense surprise long afterwards, when I was bewailing to him my parlous plight, he took me to the garret-chamber which he occupied with all the paraphernalia of his business, and going to his box produced a bagful of sovereigns, out of which he asked me to take what would satisfy my urgent needs. Of course in a work of fiction I should have refused with many high falutin' words, but being cast in a lower mould I accepted, after I had got over my amazement that he should have any money at all, much less all that, for there was well over £100 in the bag.

But I must not make this chapter too long, and so I will leave over for the commencement of the next my dealings with my dear friend, Emanuel Hauri, whose end was peace.

# CHAPTER XIX

## CONCLUSION

THIS loving stranger in a strange land was consumptive, racked with an awful cough, and lived like a dog—aye, worse than many dogs I know. By all theories he should not have lived a year, for in addition to his dreadfully disabling disease and his manner of living, he worked like an over-powered machine. He was never in bed after three in the morning, and I have known him to trundle a barrow containing a cartload of bedding plants from Covent Garden to Kilburn before beginning his work at six o'clock. And he was never fretful, never captious. The only criticism I ever heard him make was once when he told me he had employed a young Englishman to help him at a big job of work at a gentleman's garden which he was reconstructing. "He stand an' vatch me wile I do de vork, he vants 'is beer efery few minutes, he don't know dis and he von't know dat, an' at last I gif him his day's money an' dell 'im to go, for I can get on better vithout 'im. Dese people in dis country do not seem to know vat vork is ! "

284

And oh, my countrymen, is this not the case in a nutshell ?   It has got to such a pitch now, in this dear land of ours, that a pauper feels that he confers a favour upon a workhouse by condescending to board in it, and if it does not suit him he will instruct one of the labour members to ask a question about it in the House of Commons.   Poor Emanuel couldn't understand it anyhow, and I have recorded his exact words wrung from the gentlest of souls.   However, what he said to me about others is one thing, what he said to me about myself and my unbusinesslike habits is another.   But he always added " of course you are English, and do not know the need for economy such as we on the Continent have drilled into us from our earliest years.   So I don't blame you.   But I tell you that the day is surely coming, when you, all of you, will be reduced to doing what we have so long been obliged to do, gather the weeds of the field to stay your craving stomachs, and your women will have to work like ours.   I am sorry, for you have been a great people, but you have been a friend of every country but your own, and your people are getting played out —no patience, no stamina, no savvy ! "   I have translated his quaint words, but that is the sense of them, and shamefacedly I have to admit that they are scarcely exaggerated, they are nearly true.

Now this poor consumptive, who always looked more fit for an hospital than to be about at his strenuous work, had deep within his heart the passion of love, and very wrongly of course, in defiance of all right reasoning, married the girl of his choice in his youth. She came from America at his bidding, and together they lived a more strenuous life than ever, producing several children, and yet such was their united energy, always getting on. They bought a large house in Maida Vale that was running to seed, and letting it out in furnished apartments, while living themselves in a basement, made it pay.

It was at this time that I came along with my repayment of the loans made years before, and no memories of mine can overtop in interest those of the evening when I came and poured into the wife's lap the little heap of gold which represented his advances to me and substantial interest thereon. It happily came at a time when their affairs were under a shade, it was entirely unexpected and so grateful. Her face was streaming as she gathered up the coins, and said to her husband in their own language, " This makes all right, beloved one, no need to worry now."

It was a happy evening, but over it was the shadow of death. Not many weeks after I was called to his bedside, where he lay ardently desiring release from his sufferings, and assured that his lingerings here could only mean an additional burden on his wife, already staggering under a far too heavy load. I can never forget his panting words to me, " If I could only die. I have done with this world, I am of no more use here, and why I should live on puzzles me. I will so gladly go and rest." I bade him farewell and left him, to hear the next day that he had gone to that rest which he so ardently desired.

Now, I might if it were desirable give a great many more instances of the delight and satisfaction I had at that time, if it were not that I feel that these pages lack so plentifully that characteristic so earnestly, so eagerly demanded to-day, humour. I have no quarrel with this demand, for I love humour, and believe that no one has a keener appreciation of it than myself. But when I look at the majority of the alleged humorous productions, of the day, I am reluctantly compelled to say that I do not see where their humour lies. I will not mention any names I see at the foot of alleged humorous articles to-day, which give me a feeling of nausea, and I wonder mightily how anyone can be found to read, much less buy the futile piffle that is printed, and that, too, in our leading magazines and newspapers. One leading exception I will make and gladly break my rule for, Mr Pett Ridge, bless him, who never makes a mistake, whose humour is sweet and true, and who, I believe from his writings, all of which I eagerly read, is as good a man as they make nowadays. As I only know this gentleman by casual meetings at dinners, I cannot be accused of log-rolling; indeed, I know how he would heartily repudiate any effort of the kind on my part.

Now, in my present peregrinations in search of those to whom I was indebted, I was unable to trace two or three, notably the gentleman in the Adelphi from whom I had borrowed £10 at an interest of £1 per month. And so, when the business was over, and I visited my friend Mr Hardhat with the story of my efforts, he smiled grimly and said, " They'll suspend your discharge for two years, you see if they don't." I said nothing, because I did not greatly care ; but I felt that if they did, it would only be on a par with all that I had hitherto seen and known of the business. However we made the application for discharge in due form, presenting with it documentary evidence that all the debts had been paid, with the exception of those two or three that we could not find before mentioned, the total amount remaining unpaid being a mere trifle.

Now it seems scarcely believable, since one would naturally suppose that such an institution existed primarily for the purpose of doing justice to creditors, but the official to whom I presented the documents looked as if he had been personally affronted. " This ought to have gone through the Official Receiver's hands," he said severely. I was sorely tempted to reply in a similar manner, since his severity or otherwise mattered not a jot to me now, but I choked it down and answered mildly, " I wanted to save the creditors and myself trouble and fees and delay." To this he made no reply, but handed me my appointment for the hearing of my application for discharge.

That day came, and I again appeared before the Registrar to support my application for discharge. Now, when I had last come there, an utterly penniless man without any prospect of ever paying my debts, the public prosecutor or Official Receiver had dealt most leniently with me, had only stated the case against me of not keeping proper books of account, and of continuing to trade after knowing myself to be a bankrupt, without bias of any kind. But now that I had vindicated my right to be called an honest man, by voluntarily paying every man to whom I had ever owed anything, I was treated as a criminal. And on some technical count or other, which I did not understand, my discharge was suspended for two years. I endeavoured to protest, but was summarily silenced, and came away in a white heat of indignation against a system that under the ægis of law makes it more profitable to be a rogue than to be honest. I have no doubt that the Bankruptcy Act may theoretically be as near perfection as can be, but I am absolutely certain that in its administration it puts a premium upon knavery and crushes the honestly intentioned debtor into the dust.

My good friend, Mr Hardhat, was waiting for me when I emerged, and listened in silence while I exhausted my fairly copious vocabulary of disgust and dislike upon the whole sordid business. But he

T

laughed outright, when I stamped the dirt off my boots upon the threshold, and declared that I would die rather than enter the place again. However we parted an hour later, on most excellent terms, and from that day to this, nearly nine years ago, although I have passed the place a thousand times, I have never seen him again.

And now my narrative draws near its close. For when I commenced it, I meant it to contain only what should justify its title, " The Confessions of a Tradesman," and so I have rigidly excluded all that I felt would not rightly come under that head. I found also as I advanced with the story that, among the thousands of incidents which rushed to my mind, I was reduced to a really small selection, since I was determined to tell the truth only. And if I told the whole truth there can be little doubt that I should have got into exceedingly hot water. So as I have been badly scalded once, I feel disinclined to run any risks of a like nature, and while my determination, and indeed my compulsion to tell the truth is as strong as ever, I must tell only such parts of it as will not wring the withers of sensitive individuals, or give opportunity to any grasping ones to get at me in a pecuniary sense.

Writers of autobiography are often blamed, quite unjustly I think, for leaving out just those parts of their story which in the opinion of the reader would prove most interesting. But would it not be more just to remember that closely interwoven as our lives are with those of others, it would be impossible to go into all the details desired without involving other persons who have not the least wish that their names or their actions should be made public? Another thing which is constantly pressed by the reviewers of autobiographies is, that no man or woman can be trusted to tell the truth about themselves. That they will either naturally try to make themselves out better than they are, or in a spirit of perverse braggadocio, pretend themselves to be villains of a deep and deadly dye, when they have only been playing at wickedness.

From both of these reproaches I do earnestly hope to be absolved. I have honestly tried in these confessions to set down just what has happened in a curiously involved life, repressing many desires to be vindictive towards others or exculpatory of myself, and since I am not here to be accused of the crime of writing a novel with a purpose (which I understand is considered in literary circles to be the unpardonable sin), I may hope that some struggling tradesmen may find comfort and even amusement in these pages. That the Philistines, whom superior Matthew Arnold hated, but whom I believe to be the very salt of the earth, the dwellers in suburbia and its mean streets, may perchance recognise one of their own kindred, who is not looking down upon them from any sublime literary height, but who is one of them and entirely unashamed of the fact; these are my consolations and encouragements as I finish these pages.

And thus with all my heart and soul I wish to every man and woman who have sunk their precious little capital in some surburban shop, and are to-night, oh, so anxiously, looking for the customers to drop in who may make their venture a success, a bumper house. May you all feel that your efforts have not been in vain. When you look up at the prettily decorated window, every muscle of you aching with the strain you have put upon it during the last few days, may you feel not only a glow of satisfaction at the appearance of your handiwork, but may your souls be gladdened by seeing crowds of easily pleased customers with bulging purses streaming through your gaping doors.

THE END

www.ingramcontent.com/pod-product-compliance
Lightning Source LLC
Chambersburg PA
CBHW080549090426
42735CB00016B/3193